GIRLFRIEND 101

Getting Past the Baggage to Have the Relationship You Want

KIM BAKER

Contents

ISBN 13: 978-1-7322553-9-5

Created with Vellum

Printed in the United States of America

While this book is a work of nonfiction, names, locations, and some details have been changed to protect the privacy of the women I dated, including the few who should have been nicer.

Cover photo by AG Creative through 99designs.com

❀ Created with Vellum

Dedication

For anyone who knows finding the one is just the beginning.

Acknowledgments

Thank you

To Amy and my creative expressions class for reminding me that it's not about the performance

To Heather at Feather in Your Cap Editing for your heartfelt expertise in making this book better

To my beta readers for your honest input, without you this book wouldn't be what it is today

To Universal Spirit Center for providing me with the foundation on which many of the concepts in the book are based

To my friends, family, and friends I call family, thank you for your undying support and encouragement on the book development process and in life

To Jessy and Lisa at Belladia Marketing and Design for your friendship and your vision

To Judy for seeing me and sharing my vision for a better world

Acknowledgments

Introduction

A few months ago, nearly two years after publishing *Girls' Guide to Healthy Dating: Between the Break Up and the Next U-Haul*, a reader asked me what was next. We chatted about ideas for a bit before she jokingly suggested a book titled, "What now?" for all the women who are now in committed relationships. The premise would be you got the partner, the ring, the house, and maybe the marriage certificate, so what now? I explained that I could never write such a book because do we ever really know what we're doing in relationships? We laughed at the idea that only the female unicorn relationship genius could ever answer that question. But as time passed and I began leaning in to write another book, it occurred to me that while I may not have quick fix-it tools for dating and relationship dilemmas, I have had a couple of experiences and exposure to readings and research that have helped me learn some valuable lessons that have made me more authentic in relationships. It wasn't about changing or getting to some new place, it was about uncovering more of who I already was and allowing that to be seen and available in relationships. I then polled my readers and asked for input about what they wanted to read, and the number one challenge they listed in dating and relationships was baggage from the past. Now that I had some experience in! Thus, the lessons became the chapters in this book.

What I realized was that these lessons, or "soul truths" as I refer to them in the chapters, don't apply to just women in relationships, or to just lesbians. Soul truths are like spiritual pillars that ground each chapter in underlying beliefs, or "truths." As women, we are all evolving in how to be in relationships with others without losing ourselves. Maybe you're in a committed relationship and some issue keeps coming up and getting you stuck. Or maybe you're single and every time you start dating someone there is some major block stopping you from taking it to the next level. Or maybe you're not dating at all, but would like to be and aren't sure how to reconcile baggage from the past and open up to new relationships. Whatever your current relationship status, chances are some baggage from the past creeps into your life and plays a part in how you see yourself and your love life. If so, then this book is for you.

Section one is all about healing the baggage of the past. The baggage we carry forward from earlier in life often gets reinforced in our early relationships that then becomes a pattern. In chapter one, I address ways we carry unresolved grief and share the impact on our relationships. In chapter two I examine how this trance of ignoring our feelings leads to being out of touch with the impact of our own thoughts, feelings, and behaviors on our lives. In chapter three, I share how we fall into the victim trap and blame others for our own experiences.

Section two is about taking care of the present and the ways we lose ourselves in relationships. In chapter four, I address how we focus on the wrong things: other people, things we don't want, or our past. Chapter five talks about how ignoring our intuition further perpetuates our false beliefs about ourselves and relationships, and can lead us toward abusive relationship situations.

Section three looks at how we fail to take care of ourselves and how to empower our future. In chapter six, I offer ways we abandon our own needs. Finally, in chapter seven, I bring it all together with how our unhealthy habits develop over time and how our conditioning as women contributes to poor habits.

Along the way, there are action steps that you may wish to complete. Some of the action steps may be more relatable than others. In particular, the action steps on grief may delve into trauma that is better addressed alongside a therapist. Use your intuition to decide which action steps serve you and if only part of one rings true for you, take it and leave the rest. I'll provide some useful resources if you want to explore a particular subject more thoroughly. Join me as we journey together through the baggage into an empowered, authentic relationship with the most important person of all—ourselves.

Section 1: Healing the Baggage of the Past

Dealing with Grief

Most of us were not taught how to recognize pain, name it, and be with it. – Brené Brown, Braving the Wilderness

I sometimes look back and try to pinpoint the exact moment it was all set in motion, to find some clue in photos—a tiredness in my eyes, perhaps—to identify the precise moment when cells began turning into tumors. But there would be nothing to warn me of what would happen next.

24 months ago

"So, it's back to the doctor then?" Abby, my partner, doesn't wait for my response. "You can't keep living like this. This is no life."

And it isn't. These things growing inside me have taken away my ability to run and leave my blood cells so low in iron that walking across the room leaves my normal half-marathon-running-self breathless. I jokingly refer to myself as a vampire when I drink liquid iron three times a day, devour red meat, shun the sunlight, and my skin turns a sickly pale. Still, my ferritin level sits at eight (normal is 18-160) and my iron is 16 (normal is 30-126). I spent the past three months going to the doctor every month about the anemia, my concerns met with an explanation of scar tissue from a past surgery and an order to up my iron and retest in three weeks. Each subsequent doctor visit resulted in yet stronger pain medication and an assurance I could still get pregnant and carry a baby to full term. Then, something changed for the worse—the pain doubling me over, sinking me to the floor. My exhaustion from the anemia and pain finally sent me to a new doctor to get a second opinion.

I hobble into the new doctor's office, bent over in pain, a ripping feeling in my belly. Abby carries my medical records and recent ultrasound. During the exam, I explain everything, like how two oxycodone did nothing to touch the pain but made me sick instead, like how the pain got worse every single month, like how the anemia was getting so bad I could barely work. When he tells us what I must have already known on some level—that these tumors, though benign, have to come out, and that the only way is to take everything via a hysterectomy—I know that there will be no baby. Ever.

Afterward, as the day passes into the next, it begins to sink in that the problem with grieving a baby you'll never have is that you can't get away from babies. I never realized how much baby shit is everywhere. My doctor's office, where I continue to visit every week for the month leading up to my surgery, leaves me waiting for my name to be called in room full of women whose bodies are ripe with pregnancy. Babies on TV shows, babies in the aisles of Target, babies babies babies.

I am not sick. Not in a serious way, anyway. I am grateful for that and for all the other parts of my life. But I want a baby. Or, at least, the option to want a baby.

The hysterectomy is scheduled and for the weeks leading up to it, I realize that one day I will accept that this wasn't the path for me. I will move forward and travel and cherish my nieces and nephew and do all the things you do when you don't have kids.

Looking back, if healing from the surgery had been the hard part I would have been over it in about a month, maybe two. Instead, the surgery would be the beginning of a long journey of loss and grief leading back to myself and a new identity.

What does grief have to do with dating and relationships?

Grief sounds like a strange place to start a dating and relationships book, but all too often grief that is unresolved—from a past relationship, from the loss of a loved one, from a career or health crisis, or other type of loss—follows us right into a new relationship. Unresolved grief is when the normal process of grieving gets stalled, sidetracked, or pushed away entirely. If it's not dealt with, grief can become the biggest factor in our next breakup without our awareness. Unresolved grief is what stops us from opening up and being fully vulnerable to another person. It stops us from fully engaging in life. My unresolved baby grief affected every aspect of my life, especially my relationship. I withdrew from life, from myself, and I became passive and depressed. I felt insecure and hopeless.

In this stuck grief state, I was unable to take very good care of my own emotional needs, often took things personally, and became passive in communication. These behaviors not only hurt me, but they crippled my ability to be fully present in my relationships.

Too often, as women, we go from one relationship to another without fully processing the last one, leaving us with unresolved grief that carries forward into our next relationship.

Causes

After my surgery, my wound thankfully healed quickly. But my heart was broken, and this grief impacted every aspect of my life, particularly my relationships. Grief doesn't have to be caused by the death of a person. Some common causes of grief are:

- loss of a pet
- loss of a relationship
- loss of self
- family issues
- job loss or changes
- financial changes
- moving
- friendship changes
- health issues

Signs of grief

Some signs of grief are:

- sighing a lot
- loss of sleep, or sleeping all the time
- loss of appetite
- loss of interest in things that are usually meaningful
- feelings of hopelessness
- yearning
- anxiety
- frustration
- guilt
- difficulty being present
- questioning your purpose in life
- feeling detached from others
- profound aloneness

- headaches
- fatigue
- aches and pains
- difficulty concentrating

One of the most difficult things about going through a sad time in your life is that American culture does not prepare us for the profound impact of grief on ourselves and the world around us, or arm us with the appropriate tools to take care of each other when we are grieving. We are often largely unaware of the impact of our thoughts, feelings, and behaviors on our own lives. Unresolved grief keeps us stuck and unconscious. We live in a grief-illiterate culture that does not teach us how to support one another during grief (or even recognize it), which makes processing grief and resolving it in a healthy way extremely challenging. Unresolved grief can pile up and cause problems in relationships.

We ignore bad feelings

Grief is the normal and natural reaction to loss of any kind (James & Friedman, 2009). Grief gets stuck because we are conditioned to ignore bad feelings and put on a happy face.

My grief over not being able to have a baby didn't make sense to many people, which made me feel guilty and alone. Some people even compared my grief to "real" grief, implying my grief wasn't real, like when a loved one dies. There is no real grief versus fake grief. Comparing grief is toxic. Grief is grief. Permanently losing the ability to have a baby, something I had finally embraced, elicited a deep sadness. It cut across my beliefs about my purpose in life, my purpose as a woman, and my role in my family. All that sadness combined with changes in my body and hormones were simply too much to wrap my head around, and it all happened at once. By ignoring my own negative feelings, I disempowered myself. Feeling disempowered often equates to acting disempowered. In my relationship, this looked like not communicating my needs, feelings, or boundaries, experiencing rather minor, normal miscommunications almost as trauma, and being largely unable to stand in my own skin with any sense of confidence or authenticity. In a sense, my grief, though it wasn't about the relationship, was driving the ship. And the ship was sinking.

One of the most powerful realizations I have had is that by remaining largely unaware of unresolved grief, it controls me. We can't heal what we are not aware of. Power comes in realizing that we do not have to remain unaware.

We can't heal what we are unaware of.

RESOURCE TIP: For more information about unresolved grief, go to:

https://www.psychologytoday.com/blog/fixing-families/201706/six-signs-incomplete-grief

The problem with platitudes

Whenever you say something happened for a reason, don't be surprised when I slap you in the face. That was supposed to happen.—Tweet by *Jennifer Lawrence*

Remaining a grief-illiterate nation means that we just offer platitudes to comfort people who are suffering. The problem with this approach is that offering a platitude minimizes the pain that the person is experiencing, and it sends a message that is not okay to not be okay.

One of the worst parts of grief is that it isolates us from the rest of the world. If you have experienced deep grief, you know that the inner judgment and the perceived societal judgment for being sad is isolating. Platitudes and rejection of others' suffering interferes with our ability to heal.

Built to survive

Our bodies are built to survive, and when we experience trauma, particularly when we're young, we develop ways of coping with the trauma that help us survive it in the moment like:

- shutting down
- detaching from our emotions
- getting small
- acting out
- focusing on other things as a way of distraction—
  staying busy, being out of the house, general
  avoidance, caving to addiction, etc.

Our coping strategies serve us during difficult times because they allow us to cover our deep vulnerability. Like all living things, our biology sways toward surviving at all costs. Our bodies are built to identify what is wrong, what is dangerous, and to gravitate toward the familiar. In *Meditations for Emotional Healing*, Tara Brach (2009) explains that it is our evolutionary advantage to be vigilant. When we experience something wrong, dangerous, or unfamiliar, our physiological response is fight, flight, or freeze. What happens over time, though, is that these strategies become patterns that kick into gear, and often they actually interfere with our quality of life. We can get so caught up in protecting and defending ourselves that we forget who we are underneath. Nothing negatively impacts relationships more than forgetting who we are.

For example, after my hysterectomy, I felt like something had been taken from me—at the exact moment in life I was ready for it. Because my grief wasn't around the death of loved one, I felt like no one would understand. I judged myself and focused on surviving—working, and trying to get my body back to normal. But pushing away my grief only opened up a direct route to all the other unresolved grief I had in my life up to that point. As I became even more overwhelmed, my survival instincts kicked in and I detached from my emotions so much that I became frozen in my pain.

Zombie Kim may have been shut off from heart-wrenching sadness, but I was also shut off from any joy. It was impossible to be present to anything in my life. It was as if I was living my life, but on "mute." Looking back, if I had been able to acknowledge my broken heart without judgment, ask for support without receiving platitudes, and re-ground into my body, I would have been able to move through the grief sooner. Instead, it became stuck and buried so that after a while I wasn't even aware that it was controlling me.

Soul Truth

What we Resist

PERSISTS

RESOURCE TIP: For more information about healing old wounds, listen to *Meditations for Emotional Healing: Finding Freedom in the Face of Difficulty* by Tara Brach.

Grief within the relationship

All relationships have miscommunications or issues that arise. We can also experience grief within our relationships. For example, Abby and I had plans for an evening out for our anniversary. I rented a fancy dress and made dinner reservations at a nice restaurant. As the day wore on, we barely spoke to each other. I got the feeling that she was avoiding me. My feelings were hurt and as I saw my dress hanging up in the closet, I suddenly felt like a small, silly girl who made these ridiculous plans when Abby could not care less about our anniversary, or about me. When we finally talked about it, we got into an argument that left me crying and our dinner reservation cancelled. It was not a good night.

Our opportunity to repair misses happens afterward, when both people are calmed down and motivated to learn about the experience of the other person. The morning after the failed anniversary celebration, Abby and I talked openly about what happened. While my feelings were still hurt, I wanted to understand what happened. We talked about our experiences that day and what led up to the argument. I shared how I felt ignored, which just felt awkward on our anniversary, and Abby shared that she wasn't feeling well that day. We had just returned home from a holiday visit with family the night before and she thought she was coming down with something.

So, there it was. We both had our own experience of what happened, and in the end, we were both right and both wrong. I had a right to feel disregarded and Abby had a right to feel reserved when she didn't feel well. I could have communicated my feelings with her at any time during the day, and she could have communicated how ill she felt at any time as well. Our conversation was the repair and ultimately reconnection. When our repair mechanisms to clean up misunderstandings aren't in place or one person fails to take responsibility, we cannot heal. This creates more unresolved grief. It just stacks up.

━━━

The problem with unresolved sadness is that it can turn into something else. Grief always comes out, it just comes out sideways when we don't deal with it. This looks like angry outbursts, shutdowns, the internalizing of self-hate, addictions, and other unhealthy behaviors.

The powerful part about recognizing our stories and acknowledging our unresolved grief is that it gives us the power to heal them and move forward. First, we must stop re-creating the wounds. One of the best practices for healing and releasing old stories is to practice self-love.

Practicing self-love

One of the most life-changing things we can ever do for ourselves is to process stuck grief. For my baby grief, it took a long while for me to acknowledge that what I was feeling was actual grief. Once I acknowledged my grief without judgment, I began to let all my emotions come up and get out. I read *The Grief Recovery Handbook* by John W. James and Russell Friedman (2009) and learned to create time in my day to be still enough to let whatever emotions I was experiencing come up. Once all the energy I had been spending trying to ignore my feelings was spent on going into the grief and processing it, I began to feel better pretty quickly. Over the years I have learned that grief doesn't really ever go away as if it never existed, but it can be healed in ways that allows us to feel whole again.

The first step in moving forward into more authentic relationships is to heal the past. Healing the past isn't about pushing away traumatic events that happened, whether they were as a kid in your family or as an adult in past relationships. Truly healing the past involves going into the pain and the story, rather than avoiding it, and self-soothing during our suffering. Only then can we come out on the other side of it with some perspective, forgiveness, and feeling lighter having dealt with painful emotions head-on.

Although grief can get stuck following a traumatic event, in the following exercise I recommend facing stuck grief that feels safe to explore and heal. Some deep traumas may be too painful and deep to explore alone in an exercise like this one, and better supported by a therapist or practitioner.

Reaching out for professional help is not a sign of weakness, nor an indication that you are not capable of dealing with your daily life. You wouldn't attempt to perform your own open-heart surgery, right? Enlisting an expert is equally important and necessary in terms of your mental health.

▭

Action Step: What You Can Do

Grab a journal and complete your own action step on identifying and processing any unresolved grief.

TIP: One thing that may help is first engaging in some physical activity that you enjoy. For me, it was yoga. I followed these steps and did an online yoga class at home. Afterward, on my mat, something in me broke open and I knew. The baby grief was where I got stuck.

1. Find a quiet place where you will have privacy and comfort. Set your intention on uncovering grief that needs to be healed.
2. Take a few deep breaths and get grounded into the floor or your chair.
3. Begin sketching or writing without any specific goal, just let your feelings flow. For me, it helps to use pretty markers or colored pencils.
4. Connect with your body and your feelings. What do you notice is coming up?
5. Just keep moving your pencil, or typing on a keyboard, without judgment and see what arises. When we get really still, the truth of our being comes to the surface.
6. Try to avoid thinking about your feelings. Instead, focus on feeling. Notice your thoughts as you would when you're meditating—like clouds floating past.
7. Set a timer for 30-60 minutes so you can let yourself lose conscious track of time. If after the time rings you still don't feel clarity around what needs to be healed, thank your body and try again another day. Trust that with stillness your body will communicate with you.

RESOURCE TIP: For more information about dealing with grief, read *The Grief Recovery Handbook: The Action Program for*

Moving Beyond Death, Divorce, and Other Losses Including Health, Career, and Faith by John W. James and Russell Friedman.

———

Summary

We live in a grief-illiterate culture. Because we don't know how to support one another during times of grief, or how to work through our own grief, many of us are holding onto stuck grief that interferes in our relationships. We're conditioned to ignore bad feelings, and tend to push them away. But what we resist only gets bigger. The path through the worst pain is directly through it. By processing grief, we can heal, forgive, and open fully to our lives.

Becoming Aware of Our Behaviors

All human unhappiness comes from not facing reality squarely, exactly as it is.—Buddha

Sometimes when bad things happen, we fall into victim thinking. We feel and act disempowered in our lives. When things happen that we feel are out of our control, we can feel victimized and lose sight of our own power in situations. One of my biggest experiences with feeling disempowered in life came in a profound intersection of crisis in my life—I lost my job, two relatives, and a sense of who I was all within a few months. Just when I thought things couldn't get worse, life happened again.

My victim experience

I am sobbing, hands clinging to the chapel pew in front of me. I heave uncomfortable, ugly-crying sobs alone in the hospital chapel. How did it come to this? All I can think of is that there is nothing. I envision myself driving to the Coronado bridge, climbing over the railing, and flinging myself off into the San Diego Bay below.

___

Three days earlier

I am sitting in the emergency room alone, elbow on my knee, listening to the sound of the beeping machines around me. My partner, Lindsay, is for the moment away getting an X-ray, leaving her bed empty. This is how I find myself one late December evening alone and facing the news that my partner has a very serious illness. I lean back into my uncomfortable plastic chair and let out a sigh. My head is spinning. What will the treatment be? How will I ever take care of her when I am nearly falling apart myself? After the economy tanked, like so many other Americans I found myself laid off and looking for a job. Everybody, it seemed, was looking for work. Still I found a job, albeit a step down both in title and in salary, but it was a job and I was grateful. A few months in, I began to notice there was a toxic communication thread that ran through my department. More specifically, there were two toxic managers in my department who had a tendency to stretch the truth, and I reported to both of them. I had never been in this situation before, where my boss, or bosses in this case, were not honest, and prone to blaming others for their incompetence at times. In fact, it took me months to realize that maybe everything was actually not my fault. So, I had gone from a layoff to being thrilled to find a job to the increasing stress on me from having said toxic job, to right up to this afternoon when I received an urgent phone call from Lindsay. I was exhausted from the chaos and stress. I didn't know it at the time, but I had a lot of unresolved grief around losing my job.

Having been in crisis mode for the large part of the past year due to the layoff and the new job toxicity, I launched into doing things that needed to be done. First, I called her family to let them know we were in the emergency room and that I would keep them posted of her diagnosis. I promised them I would stay with her. Then I called a couple of our friends, where I very flatly relayed the information and showed little to no emotion. I think back on those phone calls now and realize that I must have been partly in shock but also desperate to have somebody ask, *Can I come support you? So you're not alone in emergency room?* Looking back, I wonder if some friends did offer and I simply couldn't take it in at the time. I didn't find the words to ask for support, either.

A few days later, after her first procedure, after her family arrived and went home, I sat in her room and listened to her breathing. I tried going home for a few hours the first couple of days, but she couldn't sleep. I stayed at the hospital all day for ten days. A few days in, I was sick with a respiratory infection myself, most likely from my long night in the emergency room that first night. In the quiet of one of the afternoons when she had finally fallen asleep, I stared off into space. I had to tell my toxic bosses that I wasn't coming into work for a few more days, knowing that I didn't have the time off and I would be paying for it when I got back to work. Everything suddenly felt like it was closing in on me, and the aloneness that I felt in the hospital room in that moment was the most profound aloneness I have ever experienced. I was not okay. I had visions of driving to the Coronado bridge and jumping off. The truth is, I was just too tired and sick to do much at all. And I was totally and completely alone. I slipped out the door and found my way to the hospital chapel. I thought maybe the quiet and peacefulness would bring me some solace.

What happened instead is that something broke open and I let myself fall totally and completely apart, resulting in heavy, wailing sobs. I kept thinking to myself I should worry about someone coming in, or disturbing someone, or Lindsay waking up and finding me not there, but I couldn't care in that moment. I had survived the layoff by getting another job. It was still an awful situation. My life was falling apart around me. Now not only was I afraid of losing my partner, but I realized I had created a life where I felt I had zero support other than her, and I had no clue where to begin to ask for it.

The good news is that Lindsay eventually made a full recovery. Our relationship ultimately didn't work out, but she is healthy and thriving today.

We lose awareness of our thoughts and feelings

Looking back, I can see so clearly now that I tried incredibly hard at everything in my life during that time period. I lost my job. No worries, I got contract work almost immediately. Then I got another job. Check. Toxic bosses. I tried harder, worked longer, took the blame for everything. Check. Lindsay got sick. I leapt into caregiver mode, taking care of everyone to the point that I got sick myself. That moment in the chapel it all came to a head. I felt like life was happening to me, and that more and more, things were being taken from me. I had no sense that I held the power over my reactions to each situation. I had cut off my emotions so strongly that I felt nothing, and at the same time thought it was a good idea to jump off a bridge. We become unaware of our feelings because we develop tools for coping with difficult emotions that largely cut ourselves off from them.

Dr. Harriet Lerner, author and psychotherapist, explains that it is not fear that stops us from doing the brave thing in our lives. She describes the problem as avoidance, and explains that our desire to be comfortable is so great that we avoid doing or saying the thing that will evoke fear and other difficult emotions

(Lerner, 2014). This is exactly what I did during my dark year. I avoided feeling bad and just kept going harder, resisting what was happening even more, ignoring my emotions and physical body until bam! I was a puddle on the floor of a chapel in a hospital with such a profound sense of aloneness I could barely breathe.

We are habitually unconscious

That moment in the chapel became my wake-up call. Up to that point, I remained largely unaware of my own thoughts and the role they played in my behavior. I suddenly realized that my habit, both in life and in relationships, was that when things got hard, I tried harder. I didn't realize that the harder I tried, the more focused I got on my end goal and the further I got away from my thoughts and feelings. The problem with trying harder, hanging on tighter, from a spiritual perspective is that it's really about resistance. Whenever we dig our heels in and try harder, we're actually resisting whatever is happening in the moment, which makes it nearly impossible to be present for it.

When I first got laid off, had I been able to stay out of fear long enough to go into the heartbreak of getting laid off despite an excellent performance record, I might have grieved and come out healthier. Instead, I judged myself for my own suffering, telling myself lots of people in the US were getting laid off, my organization closed down two offices entirely, and many of my colleagues were in much tighter financial circumstances than I. I talked myself right out of feeling what was a normal reaction to hard circumstances: anger, grief, and sadness. I became detached from my emotions and they were buried but ruled me. All that emotion was still there, just hidden. Then by staying unaware of it, I allowed the toxic new job stress and my partner's illness crisis to just pile right on top of it. I was in a cycle of ignoring all emotions. It took thinking that jumping off of a bridge was a good idea to wake me up.

Shortly after this incident, I sought help for depression that included seeing a therapist, medication, and a lifelong commitment to being aware of the way stress impacts my mental health. Depression has such a stigma that I told no one what I was going through, which only prolonged my depression and shame. As I got treated, I put the suicide hotline number in my phone. Today I am proud of this and feel no shame about it. In the end, I wanted to live more than I wanted to quit.

If you or someone you know is suffering, help is available.

RESOURCE TIP: For more information on help with depression and suicidal thoughts, contact the National Suicide Prevention Lifeline: **1-800-273-TALK (8255)**

We are unaware of the impact our thoughts and feelings have on our own lives because we often move through life habitually unconscious. For example, I arrived in the chapel that night in the condition I was in solely because I had been burying my head in the sand about the toll stress was taking on my body and soul. I was so busy *doing* that I lost all attachment to my feelings.

This quality is supported by our culture and can help us survive conditions like trauma or overcoming adversity of any type. After all, in a crisis, it is a survival tool to be able to put emotions aside and think clearly, to get away from the danger.

There is also nothing wrong with being an achiever. What I realized is that it's only when trying hard begins to override every single thing in my life, leading me to ignoring my mental and physical health, that I'm causing myself more of a problem. When it becomes a habit to dig in, hang on tighter, and try harder, I have a tendency to fall down a rabbit hole of stress. By consciously trying to be aware and present in myself in any circumstance, I have a better chance at recognizing the signs of these habits before they take over. We cannot change what we do not acknowledge. The first step in taking our power back in our habits and behaviors is to acknowledge what is happening in those moments.

Soul Truth

Awareness

is our

power

Becoming Aware

One of the biggest challenges in becoming aware of our behaviors is that they're often happening far behind the scenes in our subconscious mind. How does all this shutting off from emotions relate to dating and relationships? Nothing has a more profound impact on our interpersonal relationships than how in touch we are with ourselves. In fact, some thought leaders say that our relationship with ourselves is all there is. Once we push away our own emotions, we are simply frozen and unable to co-experience life with someone else in any real way.

Shutting ourselves off from our emotions can play out in other ways besides digging in and resisting what's happening, including being afraid of getting close to people, being too dependent or codependent, being distractible, or escaping.

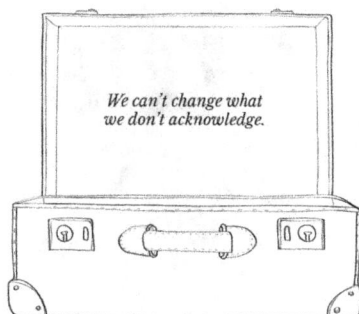

We can't change what we don't acknowledge.

Becoming aware of our criteria

When we become more aware of our behaviors, we can better notice our repeating patterns. In *Getting Past Your Breakup*, author Susan J. Elliott (2009) explains that by identifying our patterns in relationships we can empower ourselves to make profound changes to avoid repeating them.

One of my repeating patterns was that my criteria for dating was completely off. When I was in my 20s, my criteria for my girlfriend was that she was really cute, had a certain swagger, and was generally kind and funny, thus I ended up dating Lindsay, who was a good person but not really capable of being there for me in tough times. What happened with me about a year after Lindsay's recovery illustrates this point.

The situation reversed

A year later, I am sitting upright in a hospital bed, very sick, trying not to heave. The nurse pushes a liquid into my IV that I feel instantly as cold. "This should help the nausea," she tells me, her eyes empathetic. I don't remember all of the details of the first few hours of being in the hospital violently sick, except that I couldn't sleep because I was too nauseous. I couldn't drink water because I would throw it up, and I couldn't take any pain medicine because that would come up, too. There was nothing to do but endure. What I do remember is that by six o'clock that night, Lindsay had gone home, leaving me alone in a hospital room.

While there wasn't anything that she could have done to ease my nausea, I couldn't help but notice the stark contrast with what I had just supported her through a year earlier. I told myself I didn't deserve her attention in the same way because I wasn't as ill as she had been. I told myself she meant well and just got more stressed out than I had. In the morning, when I finally began to feel better, my heart was broken. Looking back, I realized that when Lindsay and I began dating we had a lot of fun together, a lot of adventures, and a connected intimacy. But within the first year of our dating life, she lied about having feelings for someone else and broke my heart for the first time. Fast forward three years and an IV full of anti-nausea medicine, and

I realized this was the worst timing ever to find out she could not be there for me.

I didn't know it then, but this moment would become pivotal in my dating and relationship life. I didn't know that Lindsay couldn't come through for me until I was literally the most vulnerable I had ever been in my entire life: sick and helpless in a hospital bed. The question that would play in my mind for months after this moment was, "Why didn't I know this about her the first three years of our relationship?"

I can tell you my exact criteria for falling in love with Lindsay: she was cute, and I was immediately attracted to her. It didn't occur to me the first time I slept with her, or told her I loved her, or met her family, that I was essentially choosing my who-to-call-in-an-emergency person. My person. The person who would be my advocate while I lay helpless in the hospital. It just never occurred to me that being hot wasn't the same as capable of taking care of someone other than herself. Because I became detached from my thoughts and feelings during the course of our relationship, particularly around the time of my layoff, I was numb to the reality that while Lindsay was (still is) a great person, she'd never be able to care for me the way I wanted and deserved.

Dating and relationships are a lot like customer service. You don't really need to know how customer service handles things when everything goes as planned. What you really want to know is what will happen when something goes wrong. How will they fix it? The same is true in dating and relationships. What you really want to know is not how someone will be when life is going smoothly. What you really want to know is how someone will be with you during hard times. Because I was so unconscious in my own life, I didn't realize I was with a partner who couldn't meet me halfway until the worst moment. It was my responsibility that I had become passive and stayed unconscious.

I want to pause here and mention that while the story is difficult for me to reveal, it is important to me to be authentic about my experiences with patterns. In that spirit, it is also important to avoid living in blame them playing the victim in my life. We will examine that more in the next chapter, but for now I challenge you to commit to taking care of yourself by raising your awareness about your own behaviors.

Action Step: What You Can Do

Grab a journal and complete your own action step on raising your awareness and identifying patterns you have ignored in relationships.

TIP: It might help to listen to a guided meditation on loving kindness or mindfulness. These types of short meditations can be found on YouTube.

1. Find a quiet, private place, and take a few deep breaths to get grounded.
2. Commit to noticing whatever comes up in the moment without judgment.
3. Think back to a situation in your current or past relationship where you felt disempowered.
4. Breathing deeply, let all the emotions of the situation arise within your body. Don't hold back. Pause and notice what is happening in your body. Notice the physical sensations and their locations. For me, it's usually a sinking feeling my chest.
5. Breathe deeply. Assure yourself that you are safe and okay and can experience suffering and heal.

6. Ask yourself what was familiar about that feeling. Was it betrayal? Was it feeling unimportant? Continuing to breathe deeply, allow whatever emotions are present to emerge fully. It may help to put your hand over your heart. Jot down your feelings and reactions to the experience.

7. Staying fully present with the feelings, see if you can identify other relationships or other times you had this feeling. What were the circumstances? What were you thinking or feeling about yourself? How did you participate in your own experience? For example, I had a tendency to ignore things as if they weren't happening—I became passive rather than engaged in my own life. These kinds of experiences tend to get bound together in a sort of ticky tacky substance in our consciousness that become patterns.

8. Continue to breathe deeply and assure yourself that you are ok and safe to explore painful memories.

TIP: If you are familiar with tapping, it can help to practice thymus tapping during this portion of the exercise.

- Take a few more deep breaths and read through your words to see what patterns emerge. Is the feeling you keep experiencing one that began as a child? Were the choices you made in how to handle it similar to the ones you made as a kid? What were you resisting about the situation?

- To take it a step further, establish a daily habit of raising your awareness. Take a mindfulness class, attend a seminar, or read a book.

▭

RESOURCE TIP: For more information on finding supportive courses and seminars, go to multiversity at: https://1440.org/.

▭

Raising our awareness

My innate, lifelong pattern of digging in and trying harder was not serving me in life and I needed to make a change in order to interrupt the pattern. That change came in the form of a crisis —getting sick. In the end, our awareness is our power. By noticing our thinking in moments, by saying to ourselves, "Here's what I would've done in the past, and here's what I want to do differently," we can both interrupt our subconscious habits and raise our awareness to what's happening in the moment.

Caution: keeping the focus on ourselves

Raising awareness is not about pointing out someone else's behaviors to raise their awareness about themselves. It's an inside job. It's on us to check ourselves about our own awareness about behaviors.

One of the best ways we can check ourselves is by being honest with ourselves about how we're really feeling. This means not only trusting ourselves in situations, but also trusting the right people.

We can also get real about our motivations and what is really driving our behaviors. For example, these days, when a crisis or challenge happens, I still have a tendency to launch into doing mode and not show vulnerability. But because my awareness is raised around this issue for myself in relationships, I can catch myself a little bit sooner. I can ask myself why am I running errands over lunch when what I really need to do is call someone and ask for support. This simple small change can have a profound impact on moving our life forward in the ways we want.

What I realized over time was that by hanging on tighter and trying harder, I was actually just completely avoiding the issues, no matter what they were. Fear may have been at the root of my tendency to dig into relationships and mindlessly try harder, but so was my deeper desire to avoid the real issues. Instead of pausing and having the courage to have real, open communication about how I was feeling, I often avoided vulnerability by instead focusing on dancing around what I wanted.

One of the most powerful tools in mindfulness is to examine our thoughts, feelings, and behavior, without judgment.

―――――

Action Step: What You Can Do

Grab a journal and complete your own action step on catching old patterns sooner.

1. Using one of patterns you identified in the earlier action step, jot down a commitment to yourself to catch yourself sooner when this pattern emerges in your life.
2. Recall the thoughts and feelings you had about yourself when the pattern emerged. For example, when I became small or invisible in my relationships, the thought I had was, "It doesn't matter what I say," or, "I don't really care enough to speak up."
3. Begin paying attention to the thoughts and feelings you have about yourself within the pattern. Check in with your body frequently and see what arises.
4. Practice tuning in to what is happening rather than tuning out.

—

Choosing to stay connected to ourselves

Years ago, scientists examined thousands of effective teachers to identify the factors that made them so successful. Researchers looked at education, age, income, credentials, socioeconomic status, family background, and other factors. After countless hours of data collection, they found one single factor determined the success of a teacher in the classroom: *Withitness.* That is, teachers who are aware of what's happening in all aspects of their classrooms the majority of the time are said to be "withit." After many years and many hard life lessons, I now appreciate the significance of withitness, whether in teaching or in dating. Being withit is really about being connected to ourselves, to our bodies, and being fully present in the moment.

Here are four ways to connect to ourselves:

1. Dial in to ourselves

Often when we feel stress or overwhelm, it's easy to tune out instead of dialing in. When we fail to monitor our own feelings and needs, we inevitably miss red flags in others. Practicing mindfulness meditation, having some healthy self-care habits in place, and slowing down a bit all help us connect to our own emotions. By dialing in to ourselves, we're better able to notice what's happening around us.

2. Pay attention

Paying attention is about noticing what's happening with ourselves. Noticing internal signals instead of ignoring them helps us honor ourselves. Paying attention also helps us know what is appropriate and what is not, and how to identify red flags when they appear.

3. Be honest

Sometimes we get into dating and realize we're not really that interested in someone. How do we tell her without hurting her? The answer is by being honest without over explaining. Saying, "What I can offer you is friendship," is clear and as kind as possible. Being honest with ourselves and with other women can stave off a lot of drama.

4. Focus on ourselves

Focusing on ourselves doesn't mean being narcissistic or making everything about us. It means keeping our energy directed at being authentic rather than trying to get her like us. Too often, when we're on a date and nervous we spend so much time worrying if she likes us that we forget to stop and ask ourselves if we like her. When we relax and focus our energy instead on how authentic we're being, we're more likely to find compatible women and have more fun in the process. This happens in established relationships, too, where we get so focused on the relationship or our partner that we fail to stay tuned in with ourselves. The term "withit" may have started in education, but it also applies to dating and to love. After all, how withit we are in life is likely how withit we are in dating and relationships.

———

RESOURCE TIP: For more information about becoming aware of your behaviors, read *The Gifts of Imperfection: Let Go of Who You Think You're Supposed to Be and Embrace Who You Are* by Brené Brown.

———

Summary

We are often unaware of the impact our own thoughts, feelings, and behaviors have on our lives. When we're unaware, we lose power to manage our lives and we move through the world habitually unconscious. Raising our awareness and opening to whatever is happening in the moment are two of the most powerful acts of self-love. By raising our consciousness and self-awareness, we are more empowered in love and in life.

3

Taking Responsibility for Ourselves

Nothing is more negative than complacency. - *Marianne Williamson*

In the *The Six Pillars of Self Esteem,* author Nathaniel Branden (1994) explains that in order to feel competent in our lives and deserving of happiness, we need a feeling of control over our existence. Self-responsibility is rising out of being at the effect of things. Branden attributes self-responsibility to building our self-esteem.

> To the extent that I evade responsibility, I inflict wounds on my self-esteem. In accepting responsibility, I build self-esteem.
> - Nathaniel Branden

In other words, avoiding responsibility is denying the wholeness of ourselves. The first step in taking responsibility for ourselves is to catch ourselves when we fall into the blame game.

We can't change what we're unwilling to take responsibility for.

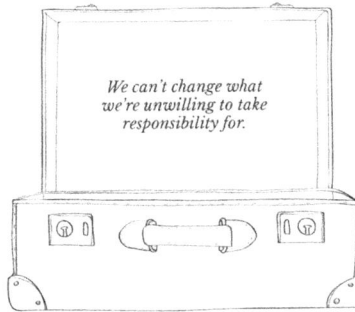

We blame others

One of the ways that we can make profound changes in our lives is to identify when we start blaming others. By blaming others, we get trapped in our own victim story. The best news is that by changing our thinking we change our lives. In *How to Heal Yourself When No One Else Can*, author Amy Scher (2016) talks about this in terms of accepting that we are part of the problem, and therefore we can also then be part of the solution.

> Being sick was not my fault, but if I wanted to get better, it had to be my responsibility. - Amy Scher

I was doubtful that just believing I could do something equated to being able to do it. But my skepticism ran deeper than just a healthy dose of critical thinking. I believed deep down that life was hard, that things happened that were beyond our control all the time, and there was nothing we could do about it. That underlying belief overshadowed smaller beliefs that came out of it. In particular, when bad things happened, especially if several happened in a row, I lost faith that we had any control over our lives. I was telling myself a victim story.

What I realized later is that while we may never have control, we can guide our lives by believing that we can change them. It is our responsibility to believe we can change our lives. I blamed circumstances (the economy tanked, and I lost my job!) and people (why couldn't Lindsay be there for me?). One of the things that happens with blame is we fall into hopelessness. Moving through life with a feeling of hopelessness is the manifestation of that belief. I thought it was Lindsay's fault for leaving me in the hospital. While she had responsibility for her choices, that pattern of feeling abandoned was entirely my own because I became unconscious in my own life and fell into the disempowerment trap.

Soul Truth

My thoughts create *my reality*

♥

The disempowerment trap

The problem with blaming others for our experiences is that it leaves us feeling disempowered. I blamed my bosses and my employer for the toxic environment they created for their employees. I blamed Lindsay for not being able to be there for me after my surgery. I blamed myself for not noticing any of it sooner. Living in this victim consciousness with all that blame and judgment only clouded my ability to know the truth. We can catch ourselves and begin to change our pattern by raising our awareness.

Practicing self-responsibility

One of the best things we can do to interrupt our disempowered feelings is to change our stories. Often, we have an experience, and we respond it to with various thoughts and feelings. Then we develop behaviors and patterns around those thoughts and feelings that reinforce the experience. The trick is to be aware of the negative reactions created by the experience, recognize them, and try to ensure that our behavior is coming from a place of conscious, positive thoughts. This happens by practicing self-responsibility and empowering ourselves. It breaks the cycle of victim thinking.

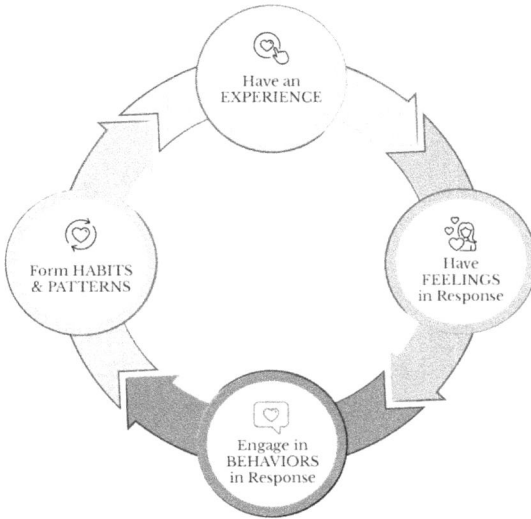

Thought cycle

Action Step: What You Can Do

Grab a journal and complete your own action step on your thought cycle.

1. Draw the thought cycle graphic in your journal. Include: an experience, feelings, thoughts, behaviors, and patterns.
2. Identify a negative experience that stands out in your mind as having an impact on your life today.
3. Begin completing each circle. First, describe the experience, your feelings when it happened, your thoughts, behaviors, and patterns that emerged over time.
4. Breathe into the experience and accept that while this thought-become-reality-graphic has carried

forward into today, it doesn't have to continue to repeat itself.

5. Repeat the process for a positive experience as well. Accept the power of embedding positive beliefs and consider what beliefs are at play in your life currently.

TIP: Another strategy for moving through the world with self-responsibility is to identify what brings us out of our hopeless thinking or wakes us up from cycling down into hopelessness. For many people, creative arts can be an incredibly powerful tool in these moments. In particular, music, art, physical activity, being still, and being in nature are useful. In addition, meditating, taking a nap, reading, being silly, or doing anything that requires complete concentration can take us out of our toxic spiral of hopelessness.

Our part in past relationships

Another place where we have the opportunity to practice being self-responsible is owning our part in past relationships. In *Girls' Guide to Healthy Dating*, I talked about ways we shirk responsibility when we are dating like blaming the other person, making excuses for our own behavior, or minimizing our impact on others. These habits just keep us stuck in victim thinking. The truth is, we are the main character in our lives and even in our most toxic relationships where unjust things happen, we play a part in those dynamics. No one deserves to be hurt. Ultimately, we have full responsibility for ourselves and the ways in which we ignore signs of toxic relationships. One of the most powerful things we can do to take responsibility for our part in past relationships is to look back and examine places where toxic patterns emerged. In *Getting Past Your Breakup*, Susan J. Elliott

(2009) asks readers to conduct a relationship inventory to spark their own healing. The purpose of the inventory is to understand our last relationship and, more importantly, to identify our patterns in relationships. Elliott explains that this type of inventory is integral to moving on and preparing for our next healthy relationship. It can also help ensure we're not carrying forward baggage from our past relationship into the next one.

RESOURCE TIP: For more information on taking responsibility for past relationships and relationship inventories, check out *Getting Past Your Breakup: How to Turn a Devastating Loss Into the Best Thing That Ever Happened to You* by Susan J. Elliott.

Action Step: What You Can Do

Grab a journal and complete your own action step on how to identify ways to take responsibility for your part in past relationships.

1. Find a quiet place where you have privacy, and take a few deep breaths.
2. Identify a recent experience in a relationship where you feel blame and judgment for the other person. Jot down details about the experience, making sure to include what happened, how you were feeling, what you wanted and needed, what the other person's perspective was, and how the situation was or was not resolved.
3. List 2-3 places where you had a role in the situation. For example, when Lindsay left my hospital room, I could have asked her to stay. I could have called her later, when I realized how alone I felt, or I could have called someone else. None of these decisions

removes responsibility from Lindsay's shoulders. She's still responsible for leaving. But if I really want to improve my own experiences in my relationships, I need to understand why my role was, and what I would do going forward to make better choices for myself.

———

One of the biggest lessons I took away from my relationship with Lindsay was that it wasn't her fault. I had to get real about my role in the dynamic of that relationship. After some self-reflection and a lot of healing, I realized a few things.

My realizations

She treated me the way I expected and allowed her to.

Part of me always believed, deep down, that I didn't deserve to be taken care of. This was an old, false belief that originated long ago, which I reinforced by choosing situations and people who weren't capable of taking care of themselves, much less someone else. Or I'd choose someone capable but ask for nothing, refuse help in small ways when it was offered, fail to communicate my needs, and then be shocked when they weren't met. Changing this habit was one of the hardest but most life-changing steps I have ever taken.

I was the one who changed the game.

Looking back, I recall several times when Lindsay just couldn't cope with her own emotions, so there was no room for me, including when she was in love with someone else and instead of telling me she slept with her, she lied and withdrew from our relationship. Lindsay is a good person, but we weren't right together. I had expectations about what it meant to be there for a partner that I felt were violated. I needed someone who could meet me halfway, someone who was capable of showing up for me in the ways I showed up for her. At the time, though, I didn't take responsibility for myself and my relationships, and felt like life was happening to me. I fell into victim thinking full-force, ultimately because I had a toxic relationship with the most important relationship of all: myself.

A toxic relationship with ourselves

Perhaps the most powerful tool for owning our part in past relationships is to identify where and why we developed a toxic relationship with ourselves. For example, in my relationship with Lindsay, I didn't like myself very much. Otherwise, I never would have put up with the dynamics that formed over time. I never would have allowed myself to lose my voice and become passive in my own life. I had expectations about what being partners should look like that I failed to communicate, and I failed to hold my boundaries for taking care of myself.

Denying our responsibility in our own lives is the very definition of negativity.

Examining past relationships

In search of more understanding about my role in past relationships, I sprawl out on my bedroom floor with a glass of wine and old journals as my cats romp and tumble about the room. As I read my own words and remember the sweet beginnings, the vulnerable miscommunications, and each relationship's ultimate demise, I realize two things at the same time: that I never really knew what I was doing, and that anything I do know today is because of the women I now call my exes.

Here are the top four things I learned from past relationships:

1. Relationships were a mirror for how I felt about myself.

For years, I blamed my bad relationships on my exes, and then I got in the worst relationship I've ever been in. Our communication was toxic. One moment she adored me, the next moment she was emotionally abusive. When the relationship ended, I had to really look at how and why I participated in it to begin with. In the end, I realized that when we started dating, I was in the middle of a deep depression, one that left me feeling hopeless and wondering, "Who would want to date this?" I started the relationship with a victim mindset! Looking back, I recognize that in that checked-out, self-despising state, I wasn't as dialed in to compatibility, to what was or wasn't healthy, or to red flags as I wanted to be, or as much as would have been healthy for me. Our relationship was just a reflection of how I felt about me.

2. Love doesn't trump incompatibility.

In the movies, when things go awry with our leading couple there is a moment when one lover realizes that their love can overcome any challenge. Love, the message tells us, conquers all.

Cue the uplifting music as our lovers race through an airport toward each other. Or something. In real life, I've spent a lot of time in airports and the truth is, I have never seen a single person racing toward their partner. Several years ago, I met an amazing woman, Cali, who had every quality I had been looking for. Yet we couldn't really understand each other. I began to understand that, to put it in *Seinfeld* terms, we were great together on paper. As the relationship progressed and we rarely met in the middle, I began to understand relationships in a different light. It's not really about blame or being right or wrong. I realized that there was nothing wrong with her and there was nothing wrong with me, we just didn't fit.

3. Losing myself in relationships was from a lack of boundaries.

Of all the lessons I have learned about love in 20 years of dating and relationships, setting and holding appropriate boundaries has been the biggest game changer of all. Where I would have let myself focus all my energy on the relationship in the past, I learned to check in with myself about how I'm feeling, what I need, and the balance I want between taking care of myself and taking care of the relationship. I developed more skills around communicating to better take responsibility for myself. This realization helped me take ownership of my own happiness and avoid taking responsibility for things that weren't mine. The best part about learning about boundaries was that it applied in all parts of my life—with friends, at work, and with family.

4. I had my guard up in most relationships.

I often felt confused and that I was alone in relationships to deal with life when things went sideways, including with friends and family. I could never understand why, periodically, I felt supported and safe, while other times I felt like I was dangling out on a tree limb by myself. Finally, I connected that the times I felt support were the times I let my guard down. I let people in enough to see I was struggling. I didn't understand for many years that the ability to be vulnerable or not was totally in my control.

These days, I'm working on having gratitude for all the things I learned from my relationships, to take responsibility for my part in them, and to let go of anger and hurt that doesn't help or serve me today. It isn't a clear thing—some days I'm Zen about it all, and other days I feel edgy with frustration. But I'm working on it.

One of the best things about learning from our past relationships is that it allows us to examine our current habits and understand how they contribute to suffering we have in the present day.

Summary

Ultimately, we are responsible for every aspect of our lives. It is challenging to take responsibility for everything that happens in our lives. When we fall into the habit of blaming others for our circumstances, we tell ourselves a victim story. But it is empowering when we realize that we're the only ones that can make ourselves happy. Once we commit to being fully responsible for ourselves and our happiness, we are on the path to being an emotionally savvy and evolved person.

Our thoughts create our reality by becoming experiences that we re-create over and over. Only when we raise our self-responsibility can we truly raise our hopefulness and overall happiness.

Perhaps the best way to move from victimhood to a self-empowered mindset is to focus on taking care of the present, which we will explore next.

Section 2: Taking Care of the Present

4

Knowing Our Worth

You have been criticizing yourself for years, and it hasn't worked. Try approving of yourself and see what happens.—Louise Hay

Having high self-worth or self-respect is about accepting and acting on the belief that we are already whole. Nothing is broken or missing. In *The Six Pillars of Self Esteem*, author Nathaniel Branden (1994) describes self-respect as the conviction that our life and well-being are worth acting to support, protect, and nurture; that we are good and worthwhile, deserving of respect, and that our happiness is important. It is not the delusion that we're perfect, nor is it competitive.

Not long ago, I went through a phase of total writer's block. Not only was creative flow out of my reach, but I didn't want to write anything about dating or relationships. At first, I thought I was just burned out. My day job had ramped up and I had more responsibilities than ever before. I was challenged in a positive way, yet more tired at the end of the workday than I had been in a long time, leaving little room for creative flow. I thought maybe I was just done writing about dating and relationships. I thought if I tried a completely different genre like fiction or children's books I'd get my creative flow back. Nothing.

For about a year, I lost all interest in writing, in promoting my book, or in thinking about the next one. Then an opportunity came up to join a creative expressions class that was offered by my spiritual center. A group of 15 of us met with our music director and learned, practiced, and eventually performed a song. By performed, I mean singing on stage solo in front of an audience. While I love singing and have been in choirs, there really isn't a talented enough music director in the world that could make me sound good solo. After all, I was used to blending in, becoming small, and being invisible. I signed up anyway, thinking maybe I could at least break through my creative blocks. The first week we each sang a short, easy couple of lines solo while the teacher gave us feedback on how to improve. Her words were encouraging, and the class was fun. I waited to go almost last, hoping I wouldn't have to go at all. When my turn came, I was so nervous I couldn't stand still. I sang, and her advice to me was to relax. She gave me some silly phrases to say, some body movements to loosen me up, and I sang again. This time, I could hear my voice hitting the notes (at least a couple of them, anyway) solidly and confidently. The class erupted in applause, and I breathed a sigh of relief.

Our assignment for the next class was to bring sheet music for a song we wanted to perform. I picked a lullaby-like song by my favorite band. My plan was to get to class early to practice it and get the teacher's feedback on my song choice since it wasn't a familiar song. But I didn't get there as early as I would have liked, and other class members had the same idea. I sat in the back row near the door. In a tiny room full of people, I felt most comfortable with a little breathing space. Just before class started, someone sat in the chair right in front of me and blocked my view of the teacher. I spent the rest of the class trying to see around her, moving my chair slightly to the left and craning my neck, but inevitably felt there just wasn't room for me. I could have moved, but I didn't.

This is where the body comes in. Had I checked into my body in that moment, I would have felt a familiar sickening feeling of an ugly old belief: I am invisible and there is no room for me. When it was my turn, I fumbled with the pages of sheet music and couldn't find the words or a single note. I was humiliated and devastated. I held back tears as I returned to my seat. I don't mind not being a good singer, but I didn't need more experiences that reminded me that I'm alone in the world. Nor did I need more experiences reinforcing my belief that I'm invisible.

We focus on the wrong things

I had a breakdown on the drive home, crying, asking God why he put me here only to be alone in life. This moment was a dark night of the soul experience. I sat on my kitchen floor and cried for all the times I felt invisible, like there wasn't room for me. I felt so stupid for believing that I could change that. I remembered so clearly being alone through Lindsay's hospital stay, my breakdown in the chapel, being alone when I was left in the hospital, and all the other times I felt profound aloneness. I felt convinced that it was my lot in life to move through the world alone. I told myself that no matter what, I wasn't going to subject myself to more humiliation or experiences of aloneness. I would take care of myself in that way.

The next morning, I still felt heaviness in my heart, but I also felt something else: curiosity. Was it a coincidence that the very thing that brought me to class—my desire to connect and release the old belief that I have to live in the background all the time—was coming up so strongly right now? I decided this experience was an opportunity to practice letting people see who I am, to let my guard down just like all my classmates were doing each week. I spoke to the teacher about my experience, and thankfully she was kind and gracious and suggested a new song that was simply titled, "How could anyone?" I looked up the song on YouTube.

> *How could anyone ever tell you, you were anything less than beautiful? How could anyone ever tell you, you were less than whole? How could anyone fail to notice that your loving is a miracle? How deeply you're connected to my soul.*—Libby Roderick, *Turtle Island Records*

The words resonated with me immediately, and the melody was simple and lovely. I went back to class the following week, and week after week experienced more support and love than I have ever received. I realized it was never about the singing—it was about coming out of the background and letting myself be seen. I had to have the ugly night to break through my walls about receiving support.

The night of our performance was magical. We were all dressed up and met at a school for our performance. After some vocal warm-ups, we sat in the front row while guests arrived. I was so touched when a friend I invited arrived to support me that I leapt up from my seat to give her a hug. During the performances, my classmates and I cheered for each other, clapping and standing up. Every performer was brilliant. The audience loved it. When it was my turn, I took a deep breath, walked across the stage, introduced myself, and explained that I took the class to break through writer's block, which happened. But what I didn't expect to happen and what I got out of the class was an awareness that I was living in the background and it was time to come out of the shadows.

As I sang, I pretended I was singing to my class as they all sat in the front row smiling up at me. I was so present and aware of the love in that room that I realized I had never fully let myself receive that kind of support before. For once, I wasn't trying so hard to do it right. I sang well, and when it was over, made myself take just a second to absorb the applause, and to giggle just a little at how lovely it all was. I floated for weeks after that, convinced I could do anything. This all happened because I stopped abandoning myself and let myself receive love.

The belief that I was invisible manifested in my relationships by focusing on the other person instead of myself, and ultimately losing alignment with myself and my values. My story, my experiences, my thinking, my behaviors, and ultimately, my reinforcing decisions, led me to believe in the habit that I had to do everything alone.

When life happens, it is easy to forget our worth and focus on the wrong things. We lose alignment with ourselves. Rather than focusing on ourselves and our needs and feelings, we have a tendency to focus on other people, on what we don't want to happen, or on the past.

RESOURCE TIP: For more information about finding out who you are, read *The Six Pillars of Self Esteem: The Definitive Work on Self-Esteem by the Leading Pioneer in the Field* by Nathaniel Branden.

We lose alignment with ourselves

Almost everything in life comes down to knowing and loving ourselves. Sometimes in dating and relationships, we lose alignment with ourselves and forget why we're here. By knowing ourselves, we are able to identify how we feel, what we need, what our boundaries are, and how to communicate them accurately and consistently. Knowing ourselves allows us to ask for help and support when needed and pushes us to own our happiness in every situation of our lives. One of the most empowering things that happens when we get in touch with ourselves is that we are aware of the patterns that we hold in our lives and our relationships. Also, we can better take care of our own needs by feeding our hobbies, addressing our feelings, and spending time with friends and family for support.

Whatever our level of self-worth, our lives will create and reinforce it. To increase our self-respect, we have to do things that cause it to rise. This begins with a commitment to loving ourselves.

Soul Truth

Everything
comes down to

---

knowing
& loving

OURSELVES

Getting to know ourselves

Knowing and loving ourselves is really about committing to ongoing growth no matter where we are in life. Part of this awareness is acknowledging what needs work within ourselves. It is a delicate balance between accepting ourselves as we are—faults and all—and continually learning and expanding more into who we are meant to be. Books, classes, workshops, and webinars are all part of maintaining our ongoing awareness in relationships.

RESOURCE TIP: For more information about improving your relationships by getting to know your yourself, go to Katie and Gay Hendricks's course "Attracting Genuine Love" at:

http://www.heartsintrueharmony.com/catalog/attractinggenuinelove.html

Is she capable?

Another important piece of knowing ourselves is recognizing when someone else isn't capable of growth or unwilling to grow. This can be tricky in a relationship because two people have their own needs and their own experiences, yet these needs and experiences intertwine in a delicate dance that we call emotional intimacy. How do we know if someone is incapable of growing or is unwilling to grow? The way I have answered this for myself is to do three things:

- **Watch her behaviors over time**. Does she have a pattern of an inability to say "I'm sorry"?
- **Ask: Is she able to own her part in misunderstandings?** Or is she prone to

projecting, blaming, or toxic behaviors such as gaslighting, lying, erupting into a rage, or withdrawing?

- **Ask: Is she able to communicate through conflict?** Is she able to have an open, calm conversation about conflict?

Another piece in knowing ourselves is knowing what we need to feel the most like our true selves. For example, when I first came out, I was 26 and living in a conservative part of the country, working in a conservative job. I did not know a single person who was gay, and so I floundered around for a while believing that I had to join a softball team and dress in khakis and plaid shirts in order to be in a real lesbian. Luckily, a gay male friend confronted me and asked, "What are you doing? This isn't you. Are you dressing like this to prove you're lesbian?"

I defended myself in the moment, but I thought about it later and realized I didn't know how to dress for me—I didn't know who I was. So, I began to find out. (This was the beginning of my lifelong love affair with high heels.)

Triggers

Another component of knowing ourselves is recognizing what our triggers are. A trigger is an experience that is reminiscent of an old, painful experience that we once had. This is more than just recognizing our boundaries and deal breakers. Our triggers are things that we are particularly sensitive to—more than the average person—because of our history with our families, our past partners, and the stories we have developed or told ourselves around those events.

Triggers can be unhinging. I recommend choosing something less charged than a deep trigger for the following exercise.

Action Step: What You Can Do

Grab a journal and complete your own action step to identify some of your top triggers.

1. Identify a situation with an ex or current partner that evoked a very strong response in you. Our reactions can be good indicators that there is something more going on than what is happening in the present moment.

2. Think back to your response to the situation and identify the specific feeling you had that felt strong. For example, I found out Lindsay had kept some secrets—though rather harmless—from me, and was deeply hurt and furious. By looking deeper, though, I realized my hurt wasn't about the secrets she kept. It certainly doesn't build trust to keep secrets, but the real issue is that secrets were a trigger for me. My family didn't talk about things honestly, which meant anything that was going on with anyone, including their feelings about it, was—you guessed it—a secret. Then I dated Lexi, who lied, cheated, and gaslighted me throughout our relationship. Her way of operating was secretive even when she didn't have to be. So, secrets became a trigger for me.

3. See if you can identify 2-3 triggers. Examine issues

that arise again and again that bring out a strong emotional response in yourself. Remember that awareness is power. We can't heal what we don't acknowledge.

Reminder: Acknowledging our triggers does NOT negate another person's responsibility in a situation. We are simply looking at it as a whole and accepting where our sensitivities are so that they don't control us when we're unaware of them.

Of all the healthy habits that have a positive impact on our connection to other people, self-awareness may be the best. Being self-aware means being dialed in to our feelings in any given moment, including our needs, feelings, and stories, and taking full responsibility for them. Self-awareness is what stops us from projecting our shit onto other people. It is what allows us to open up in a conversation after a misunderstanding rather than shutting down and falling into the blame game. One of the biggest ways to check on alignment of our values with our thoughts and behaviors is to examine our boundaries.

Identifying our boundaries

You sleep with her on the first date. You commit to a relationship before you really know her. You move in with her before you've seen each other in different situations. You date more than one person but don't tell either of them. You say yes when you want to say no to commitments. You flirt with your ex. You make out with a friend. Most of us have done at least one thing that illustrates poor boundaries in dating and relationships. As a reformed no-boundary-a-holic, I look back and realize that I didn't know I had poor boundaries in dating. I didn't even know what a boundary was.

Boundaries

A boundary is the line that differentiates you from someone else. In dating, boundaries are the practice of holding that line so that circumstances or other people don't sway you from aligning your values, your words, and your actions.

Improving my ability to set and hold boundaries was the number one habit that turned my dating life around. The biggest benefit is having trust in myself to know I'll do what I say. For example, before I developed good boundaries, I said I would only have sex when I was in love. But then, because of immaturity, loneliness, or alcohol, I gave that value away by sleeping with women on the first couple of dates. I am not saying that sleeping together on a first date is wrong. I'm saying that for me, sleeping with someone on a first or second date when I made a promise to myself that I wouldn't is self-betrayal. It was incongruous with my values and my behavior that revealed my boundary violation. I had to ask myself: What is it about this situation that causes me to compromise my own values?

The importance of boundaries

Boundaries help us hold on to ourselves. Signs of good boundaries in relationships are things like maintaining your own hobbies and friends, maintaining personal values, and communicating openly. Bad boundaries in dating are things like dropping all your friends once you get a girlfriend or boyfriend, having an inappropriate relationship with your ex, or taking things outside your relationship that should stay within it, like complaining to a friend about your relationship instead of talking to your partner. The biggest issue with having poor boundaries is it often leads to self-abandonment. In my relationship with Lexi, I moved in with her fairly early on, even though my gut was telling me to get my own place. By abandoning this need in myself, I set myself up for being disregarded in the relationship and in the household. After all, I was the one who ignored my own need to remain independent.

Boundaries keep our relationships sacred. Healthy relationships are built on pillars like trust, intimacy, and respect. Part of building these pillars over time is knowing that you'll each keep relationship stuff within the relationship. For example, Lexi had a best friend whom she used to date who was still very flirty with her. It didn't bother me much until I realized that she was talking about her feelings with her ex and not with me. The person we share our world with is our person. When we shut out our partner but let someone else in, it erodes trust and ultimately the foundation of a relationship. I learned over time that a good boundary in this scenario, when you're wanting support from a friend regarding your relationship, is to avoid secrets. Anything I say to my friend about my relationship I have already said to my partner. Good boundaries help us know with certainty that we have each others' backs and engage in relationship-building habits rather than tearing-down habits.

Our role in boundaries

When my worst boundary-crashing relationship crumbled around me, I took a step back and looked at my own role and habits when it came to boundaries. I realized that practicing good boundaries in dating means going through the stages of dating rather than skipping over the main getting-to-know-each-other stage. I began to get in touch with what was really important to me and consider how I could create a boundary that protected that value. In the next action step, I share three values and how I lined them up with boundaries to be more congruent.

━━

Action Step: What You Can Do

Grab a journal and complete your own action step on determining your boundaries and how they align with your values. I provided my example to use as a model.

Value: *Getting to know someone to see if we're compatible before falling in love.*

The aligning boundary to this value was to only have sex once I was in a monogamous relationship. What holding this boundary meant was I had to place really getting to know a woman over time above anything that would sway me to have sex.

Value: *Maintaining my own hobbies, friends, and voice when in a relationship.*

The aligning boundary to this value was to continue to work out, see friends at least twice a week, and identify and communicate my feelings. What holding this boundary meant was that I had to take responsibility for keeping my schedule my own, even when trying to integrate it with someone else's. I also wanted to speak up on my own behalf and say how I felt without worrying about what the other person thought.

Value: *Being completely honest with myself and with women I date.*

Holding this boundary meant I had to get real with myself about why I was going out on a date. If it was because of boredom, loneliness, or complicated feelings about my ex, then I wouldn't go. I would only go if I was interested in the woman and wanted to get to know her better to see if we were compatible. This sounds totally obvious, but the truth is, too often I went out for the wrong reasons.

─────

Practicing good boundaries is a game changer. For me, getting my values in line with boundaries that support them sets the stage for the healthiest of relationships. Another place self-worth plays out in dating and relationships is compatibility.

Compatibility

When it comes to love, we could be with just about anyone and issues will arise. As long as we go on believing that there is a perfect person out there with whom no conflict will ever happen, or we will not ever be triggered with, we will just bounce from person to person without ever addressing our own issues. However, if we can look at love through the lens that issues will arise no matter who we are with, and our job is to open to the learning and unfolding in each moment, we can better identify what compatibility is and what it isn't.

Compatibility is rather confusing. You meet. You're into each other. Yet somehow, you're still not compatible. She has 800 Facebook friends, you have six. She likes being on the constant go, you like staying in. She is happiest when you spend six nights a week together, you're happy with three. And so it goes. Common interests and attraction alone do not equal compatibility. If not that, then who are we compatible with? What is compatibility, exactly?

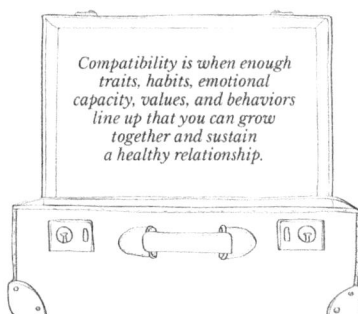

Compatibility is when enough traits, habits, emotional capacity, values, and behaviors line up that you can grow together and sustain a healthy relationship.

When I look back, most of my relationships were defined primarily by physical attraction and shared interests. The incompatible relationships were like existing in a constant state of confusion and conflict. We didn't agree on anything, from appropriate boundaries, to what is and is not respectful, to how to manage time and money. The compatible relationships were the ones where I felt like the relationship brought out the best in both of us, pushed me to grow, to learn about myself, and to step a little more into who I already was.

___

Action Step: What You Can Do

Grab a journal and complete your own action step on compatibility.

1. Find a quiet place and jot down the traits, habits, emotional needs, values and behaviors you have in common with your partner or that you would like in a partner.

Consider the following questions:

- How does she deal with her emotions?

- Is she self-aware enough to communicate her feelings?
- Does she have any red flags that seem beyond normal? (see chapter five)
- Does she make sense to me? What is needed to make sense to me?
- Can we understand each other enough to move in the same direction in life?
- Am I, or is the relationship, the first priority?

Anchors

Relationship *anchors* are the underlying questions beneath issues that arise. For example, with Lexi, when she began alternating between being highly affectionate and highly critical, I couldn't help but wonder if she really knew me. Some other relationship anchor questions are:

- Are you as interested in me as I am in you?
- Are you honest?
- Are you committed?
- Are you capable of communicating your feelings?
- Are you capable of and willing to continue growing in the relationship?

Another way to evaluate compatibility is to examine signs of incompatibility.

Signs of incompatibility

In my relationship with Lindsay, I ignored signs of our incompatibility early on. She was broody and cynical, making my joy and optimism feel silly. She wanted to see beautiful places from the comforts of a vehicle and I wanted to be climbing around in the dirt in the middle of it. In the end, all the signs pointed to the inevitable—a breakup. I couldn't help but wonder: what would it be like if I paid attention to signs of incompatibility earlier rather than waiting three years to deal with it?

Here are eight signs of incompatibility:

1. **Frustration exceeds joy**

Whenever emotions bend toward the negative more often than toward the positive one of two things is happening—either you're at a normal bump in the road, one that is an opportunity to navigate and grow together, or the stress of the relationship outweighs the benefits. How do we know the difference? It's all about patterns over time. If you're unable to repair breaks or there is a constant undercurrent of negative emotions, it's just not meant to be.

2. **Depth is limited**

In my relationship with Cali, we had so much in common that it didn't make sense why we argued All. The. Time. We both loved working out, drinking wine, and laughing at stupid funny movies. While having things in common is important, shared interests are not the glue that holds people together. What you really want to know is: *how do we navigate our differences, particularly when there is conflict?* Cali and I were great on the surface, but we just didn't have the depth together to move through life as a team.

3. **One person is in the center**

One of the biggest relationship red flags is when we become someone else in order to make the relationship work. Love is not having to play small to keep the peace or to support someone else's goals. Real love is about being a team, where both people benefit and thrive.

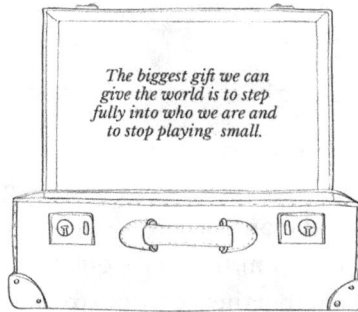

The biggest gift we can give the world is to step fully into who we are and to stop playing small.

4. You rarely understand each other

Relationships are places where we grow, not places to be told we need to change. Once we get the idea that we need to change ourselves or the other person to be in a relationship, we may want to look at compatibility issues. When Lindsay and I first started dating, I listened to her share a story about her ex and a pivotal conflict they had. I asked her what her role was in the fight and she stared at me blankly. Needless to say, a situation almost identical to this one arose in our relationship and I remember thinking, "Oh yeah, she didn't get it with her ex and she's not going to understand it with me, either."

5. You can't be yourself

Without question, every single time I have been in a relationship where I was constantly criticized for being me, I knew we weren't right together. Love isn't control. Love isn't my way or the highway. When we are truly loved and in a compatible relationship, it brings out the best in us.

6. Everything is hard

By "everything," I mean *everything*. With Lexi, we had reached a point after about a year and half of dating where we could talk about nothing except *Breaking Bad* without arguing. Anything else created friction, some kind of weird competition in the conversation, defensiveness, and this anger that I have never experienced before. These kinds of reactions can happen in healthy relationships, too, particularly when issues are unresolved or when one person feels disrespected. But generally healthy relationships are fairly easy most of the time, consistent, and allow us to be ourselves, and to feel seen in love.

7. One person is unwilling to grow

Signs of this look like an inability to say I'm sorry, emotional stoicism, shutting down, being unable to engage in conversation without being disrespectful or condescending, and a consistent inability to take responsibility for their part in the misunderstanding or the conflict.

8. Boundaries or deal breakers are broken

In my experience, when one person's boundaries or deal breakers are broken, the relationship is over. When there is a lack of respect for boundaries, trust erodes and contempt sets in.

One way to differentiate between normal relationship stuff and incompatibility stuff is to examine relationship pillars.

Relationship Pillars

Healthy relationships are built on pillars that have deeper roots than just attraction. Pillars are like cords that keep us grounded. Some pillars are: trust, having a team mindset, intimacy, respect, authenticity, communication, commitment, and passion. True compatibility is tied to these foundational pillars above all else.

Pillars of HEALTHY RELATIONSHIPS

Trust Trust is more than just having faith that she won't cheat, it's an inner confidence that she has your back. Trust involves answers to questions like: Can I know that you will tell me how you feel? Can I rely on you to hear my feelings and needs? Can I depend on you to stand up for me when necessary? Can I have confidence that you'll hold boundaries and keep our relationship sacred? To me, being faithful and not cheating are the bare-bones minimum in building and maintaining trust. When she has your back, you feel it in her actions, and in the ways she allows herself to be vulnerable and consistent over time. It's this consistency that builds a deep inner trust in knowing you're a team.

Team Mindset Another feature of a healthy relationship is that you can work as a team. One of the things I discovered later in life is that I had been solo on and off for so long in my adult life that I expected to have to do everything myself. Independence is fine, but it is another thing entirely to move through the world as a perpetually single person. Working as a team involves allowing ourselves to be vulnerable enough to ask for help, to consider what's best for the team as opposed to what is just best for ourselves, and being willing to continually look at our role in situations.

Intimacy In my experience, when a relationship isn't working even when love is there, intimacy is usually what's missing. Intimacy is more than sex or passion, it's about connection. When you share your world with her and she shares her world with you, a closeness develops. Over time, this closeness can either build or crumble, depending on how you manage your time, how you manage repairing miscommunications within the relationship, and how open you are together in difficult times. While a violation of trust is the number one intimacy killer, the number two crusher of intimacy is control. When someone uses manipulation, emotional abuse,

Pillars *of HEALTHY RELATIONSHIPS*

Intimacy
(continued)

or other damaging tactics to control the relationship, you can count on intimacy going right out the window. On the other hand, intimacy can be built in the smallest moments in life: a flirty smile after a misunderstanding, a thoughtful text message letting her know you miss her, or a surprise hour together after you've been apart. Tiny gestures can add up to big gains in intimacy building.

Respect

While respect in the professional sense means admiration, when it comes to intimate relationships, respect goes deeper. Showing respect sends the message that you matter, and it's challenging situations that demand it the most. It's easy to speak respectfully to each other when things are good. But what about arguments, misunderstandings, or miscommunications? These are all part of deep intimate relationships that last over time. Maintaining her dignity is key in expressing respect, even when your emotions are flaring. This means saying how you feel openly but without personal attacks, using a biting tone, name-calling, or shutting down. Maintaining dignity is about honoring her experience and feelings while honoring your own. It means listening more than talking. It sometimes means taking five until you're calmer and more present to the conversation.

Authenticity

One of the most important things about being in a healthy relationship is that we can be ourselves. Good relationships enhance us while supporting us and push us to be better people. The main way to check in on this is your sense of security. One of the most important foundations for security is consistency. Do you know generally what to expect from day to day? Week to week? Or is the relationship in constant flux? Communication is a great indicator of consistency and the health of a relationship. When communication is both transparent and intended to understand the other person, both people win in the relationship.

Summary

We have a tendency in relationships to focus on the wrong things: our partner, the past, or what we don't want. This focus causes us to lose alignment with ourselves. Since everything in life and relationships comes down to loving ourselves, we can turn things around by refocusing on ways to avoid self-abandonment and increasing our self-worth and self-respect. Trust, having a team mindset, intimacy, respect, and communication all depend on and intertwine with one another to create a sense of security that you're in this life together. When any one of these key pillars are broken, the difference in moving forward and ending the relationship lies in the ability to repair the damage.

5

More Than Just Issues

Psychopaths are natural human behaviorists from childhood—studying what works in motivating, conning, or hoodwinking others.—Sandra L. Brown, Women Who Love Psychopaths

Though we are responsible for all parts of our lives, sometimes in dating and relationships we come across someone who is not tethered to reality and has more than just issues. I dated Lexi, my most toxic relationship, on and off for about a year and a half. There were many signs that the relationship was toxic, like after a period of closeness like an intimate conversation or lovely day, she would suddenly become cold, distant, critical, and aggressive.

One weekend, we ran at the beach and went to the spa. Then on Sunday night it was as if a switch was flipped and she lashed out about the most trivial things. We began to put together a piece of furniture from IKEA. As we were assembling the shelves, we joked around. Something I did or said triggered her, and instead of using words to express her feelings, she turned to me, her face suddenly changing, and punched me in the arm. This was the ultimate end of our relationship. When I looked back on it later, I realized that the closeness that we had experienced over the weekend was too much for her she had to push me away in order to feel safe.

While much of this book is about identifying our own issues and responsibilities in relationships, there are times when the issues in a relationship are more than just issues. Sometimes we get in relationships that are beyond normal—toxic relationships.

Emotionally abusive relationships

In emotionally abusive relationships we ignore our gut—or intuition—and get into toxic relationships where we get abused. When we are in abusive situations, whether emotionally or physically, any unhealthy thoughts and beliefs about ourselves and about love get reinforced. My relationship with Lexi was toxic and became even more toxic over time. We went from being the best of friends who laughed a lot to enemies who didn't trust each other. I felt duped—that she had lured me in as one person but became another during the relationship. When I finally had the strength to leave for good, I learned that I wasn't alone— that this trick is actually a manipulation tool abusers use called love bombing.

Love bombing

The term love bombing refers to the manipulation tactic intended to control the relationship by brimming you with attention and admiration from the moment you meet. Typically, in love bombing, the relationships are whirlwind, and the receiver is bombarded with romantic texts, emails, long conversations, and is "bombed" into feeling more adored, more understood, and more desired than ever before. Unfortunately, there are stages to love bombing: idealization, devaluation, and then discarding.

In love bombing, the idealization phase is when we get sucked in. With Lexi it happened at my most vulnerable time, when I was under a mountain of stress, missing my support system, and she was ready to jump in. I remember thinking, "Wow, this girl asks me a lot about me." All that information was later used to help her in the next step, devaluation. Once I was dependent on her support and adoration, she could begin tearing me down easily because she knew exactly which buttons to push. Emotional distance, withholding affection, temper tantrums, and criticizing me became the norm. I was blown away with confusion and couldn't imagine what had changed. Love bombing then enters the discard stage, where the toxic person simply throws you away. Lexi stayed away from home more, and I would find out later that she began dating another woman while we were still together.

It happens when we're vulnerable

One of the reasons why we get sucked into toxic relationships is because we are vulnerable to them in some way. According to Sandra Brown, author of *Women Who Love Psychopaths*, women are drawn to toxic relationships often because they begin the relationship when they are impaired: grieving, dealing with multiple losses, long-term stress, loneliness, boredom, and residual depression or grief (Brown, 2010). In addition, many of us were conditioned earlier in life that dysfunction is normal. Toxic people are familiar to us in some way, and our biology leans us toward the familiar. Another reason why we get sucked in is that we may lack the tools and skills to know how to recognize toxic people and what to do when we do get caught up with a toxic person.

Emotional abuse

The official definition of emotional abuse is: any act including confinement, isolation, verbal assault, humiliation, intimidation, infantilizing, or any other treatment which may diminish the sense of identity, dignity, and self-worth.

Looking back on my relationship with Lexi, it hit me that I had absolutely no idea that what I was experiencing was emotionally abusive. I knew it was bad, but I thought it couldn't be abusive because I wasn't being hit. Today, the mental health community has more awareness than ever before about some patterns of emotional abuse that appear in interpersonal relationships.

Because sometimes abuse is subtler, we have a tendency to miss some of the signs.

Three signs of emotional abuse:

1. You feel constant fear.

I thought as long as I wasn't afraid for my physical safety then all was good, and whatever went wrong was normal relationship stuff. Our emotional safety is a necessity for us to feel secure. Other than the occasional fear that pops up in conflict related to our past experiences, fear generally shouldn't be present in a healthy relationship. We should not have to be afraid of saying something because we don't know how she'll react. That walking-on-eggshells feeling can be a different issue around how you each communicate, but if both people are invested and capable of improving communication skills, then that fear will dissipate over time.

2. You are given lectures.

We all say things that aren't kind or helpful in conflict, but when there is a pattern of lecture-giving, mostly about how you need to change or about what is wrong with you, then it may be a sign of emotional abuse. In my abusive relationship, the pattern became predictable. We would have a conflict or disagreement, and at the point I shared my feelings ("I felt confused when you went off with that girl for three hours at the party"), instead of listening, she began lecturing me about how she needed more from me, how I should be a better friend to my friends, or something else she felt I needed to have explained to me by her. I now understand this behavior as deflecting and maybe even projecting, but at the time it just felt random and weird.

3. You are subject to the silent treatment.

Stepping away from conflict for a time period can be the best choice at times, but when her default response to communication is an angry silent treatment for long periods of time, it may be a sign of emotional abuse. The silent treatment, or stonewalling, is the refusal to consider your partner's perspective.

It is easy to identify signs of emotional abuse when they are happening to someone else, or when they are extreme, but abuse is abuse, even if the signs are subtler. What I understand now is that while we all experience fear, moments of being told what to do differently, or live in post-argument silence, it's really the patterns over time and extremes around these behaviors that indicate emotional abuse.

Other signs of emotional abuse

- Withholding
- Isolating

- Ignoring
- Minimizing
- Chronic deceit
- Restricting
- Threatening
- Abandoning
- Raging
- Constantly criticizing
- Ridiculing
- Demeaning
- Coercing
- Accusing
- Ordering
- Denying one's reality
- Gaslighting

RESOURCE TIP: If you suspect you or someone you know is suffering from abuse help is available. Call the domestic abuse hotline at **1-800-799-7233 or go to http://www.thehotline.org/**.

Action Step: What You Can Do

Grab a journal and complete your own action step on emotional abuse and toxic relationships.

1. Find a quiet place and take a few deep breaths.
2. Think back to one of the most confusing, difficult relationship situations you experienced. It may be with an ex, with a friend, a co-worker or boss, a family member, a neighbor, anyone.
3. Jot down everything you remember about the

experience. Allow whatever emotions arise to come on fully. Keep taking deep breaths to comfort yourself.

4. Using the signs of emotional abuse listed here or in the provided resources, identify if there were parts of that relationship that were emotionally abusive, either to you or to the other person.

5. Highlight any parts of the situation that you feel fall into emotional abuse and in the margin, write the corresponding reason. For example, Lexi and I fought about a party where she left with another woman for three hours. She denied it was more than a half hour and spoke to me like I was a child. I highlighted this part of the story and wrote "Denied my reality" and "demeaning" in the margin.

6. What matters most about this exercise is not so much finding examples of emotional abuse, but recognizing the signs. Knowing the signs will not only help you know what to identify as a red flag in the future, but will also provide some clarity that what was going on was more than just regular relationship issues.

One thing to keep in mind is that just because there were examples of it in the course of the relationship doesn't mean the whole relationship was emotionally abusive. One time toxic relationships are highly likely is when we date someone with an untreated personality disorder.

Untreated Personality Disorders

Once you've been in an emotionally abusive relationship, you build a pretty good radar to detect the signs. For me, one of the flags I have learned to pick up on is personality disorders.

As a disclaimer, I am not a doctor, psychologist, or therapist. My accounts here on Lexi include my own experiences in understanding these disorders. I have made every attempt not to generalize and demonize people suffering from these personality disorders. However, I also am transparent about my experiences with women who have untreated narcissistic personality disorder or borderline personality disorder. I want to emphasize here that my experiences are with people who were not being treated, nor who acknowledged that there was anything to look at within themselves. Some people do get treated for personality disorders and lead full lives. My stories here do not diminish or minimize those who have made those decisions.

Narcissistic Personality Disorder

In recent years, much has been written about narcissism. These days, if someone is acting selfishly, we throw out, "Narcissist!" But true narcissistic personality disorder is deeper than one selfish act. In *Why is it Always About You: The Seven Deadly Sins of Narcissism*, author Sandy Hotchkiss (2003) refers to narcissism as, "the need to feel constantly important, loved ones are not allowed to have feelings of their own or expressing wants and contradict the opinions of the narcissist."

Hotchkiss refers to narcissists as emotionally crippled, who have the development of a toddler (Hotchkiss, 2003). Narcissists mentally lack a of sense of self and have an exaggerated posture of importance unrelated to real accomplishment. They have no ability to value or recognize the separate existence and feelings of others.

Nina Brown, author of *Children of the Self-Absorbed* (2008) explains:

> *Pathological narcissism is extremely immature, unrealistic, and completely self-serving with behaviors expected of children but signals immaturity in adults, such as constantly boasting or bragging, expecting others to immediately meet their demands without protest, or taking unnecessary risks that can be very self-destructive.*

RESOURCE TIP: For more information about narcissism read *Why is it Always About You?* by Sandy Hotchkiss.

RESOURCE TIP: For more information read *Children of the Self-Absorbed* by Nina W. Brown

Some symptoms of narcissism

According to the DSM IV-TSR, some symptoms of chronic narcissism are:

- Grandiose sense of self importance
- Exaggeration of achievements and talents
- Expects to be recognized as superior without corresponding achievements
- Preoccupied with fantasies of unlimited success, brilliance, beauty, or ideal love
- Requires excessive admiration

- Believes he or she is special and unique and can only be understood and associate with other high-status people or institutions
- Has a sense of entitlement, unreasonable expectations of favorable compliance with expectations
- Takes advantage of others and is interpersonally exploitive within relationships
- Lacks empathy
- Is unwilling to recognize or identify with the feelings and needs of others
- Is envious of others or believes others are envious of him or her
- Shows an arrogant behavior or attitude

Earlier I mentioned that in healthy relationships both people have a general sense of the other person's autonomy. In a relationship with a pathological narcissist, something called *fusion delusion* happens. In fusion delusion, the goal is obliteration of one partner's autonomy.

Another type of personality disorder is borderline personality disorder, which is in the same cluster of disorders as narcissism and tends to result in toxic relationships.

Borderline personality disorder

According to the DSM IV-TSR, some symptoms of borderline personality disorder are:

- Frantic efforts to avoid real or imagined abandonment

- Intense and unstable personal relationships
- Interpersonal relationships that idealize and then devalue
- Identity disturbance with unstable self-image
- Impulsivity in at least two areas (spending, sex, substance abuse, reckless driving, eating)
- Recurrent suicidal behavior, threats, or self-mutilation
- Emotional instability due to marked reactivity of mood
- Intense episodic irritability or anxiety
- Chronic feelings of emptiness
- Inappropriate intense anger or difficulty controlling anger
- Transient stress related paranoid ideas

Looking back on my toxic relationship with Lexi, I realize now that she had some traits consistent with borderline personality disorder (BPD) like unstable relationships, idealizing and devaluing partners, and problems with impulsivity. Understanding BPD symptoms and the ways they impact intimate relationships helped me understand the severe dysfunction and my addiction to it in the relationship. Lexi often exhibited what I have come to understand now as splitting. Splitting is complete black-and-white thinking.

In relationships, the partner to the BPD is often either an innocent angel or a complete monster in their minds. There is no in between and there is no reasoning about it. As a partner, I was either loved or hated. When I was loved, I was totally and completely adored, sucked into the belief that I was her "one." But when I was hated, it was the worst make-me-feel-like-a-crazy-person feeling ever. What did I do to deserve such hatred? Once I asked what time we were leaving for a road trip after I had taken the day off and she kept working well past the end of my regular work day. She didn't speak to me the entire weekend. Another time I didn't warn her that the food in her fridge was getting older and would need to be thrown out if she didn't eat it. (You read that right, <u>her</u> fridge.) What was my punishment during these hatred times? Once it was to yell at me and tell me I was a hothead (project much?). Another time it was my birthday and after failed promises to go to the beach, she locked herself in her room, leaving me to drive to the beach alone. Another time I was no longer "allowed" to park in the driveway. The punch in the arm was just a slight escalation of all the other punishments, but it was the final straw.

⊏⊐

Relationships with Women with Untreated Personality Disorders

One of the biggest challenges is that generally narcissists will not seek treatment, as the more narcissistic they are the more rigid and resistant they are to change.

This symptom is common in both borderline personality and narcissistic personality disorders. While some people successfully seek treatment, because the key characteristic of the disorders is skewed perceptions and avoiding self-responsibility, many times they won't get treatment. Because of this, confronting them rarely works.

Why does it matter what it's called?

If toxic behavior is toxic behavior, how is it useful to identify characteristics of specific disorders? While general assholeness happens in dating and relationships, personality disorders bring with them a particular flavor of toxic that can be long lasting, deep, and play on all of our existing wounds. Sometimes women who have been victimized in these relationships feel empowered as they begin to untangle exactly what happened. Understanding pathological disorders, their symptoms, and the ways we get sucked in and addicted to them, can help us process all of the emotional fallout. For example, after I began to move on from Lexi and had space to heal, I recognized the symptoms of BPD and knowing them helped me see the crazy feeling I had in the relationship as part of the disorder. It was Psychology 101.

Also, narcissism and borderline personality disorder are most often associated with impulsivity problems, interpersonal exploitation, cognitive distortions, low/no empathy, and varying levels of inappropriate/non-existing conscience and remorse, sometimes called low empathy spectrum disorders that mean inevitable harm for those who engage in close personal relationships with them (Brown, 2010). The particular damage experienced in a relationship with a person who has pathological narcissism or pathological borderline personality disorder is unique. For example, according to Sandra Brown, author of *Women Who Love Psychopaths* (2010), these two personality disorders share coping mechanisms like:

- Chameleon-like behavior
- Blaming
- Over entitlement
- Victimizing relationship exploitation
- Tiptoeing due to hyper sensitivity within the relationship
- Master-level projecting
- Creative splitting
- Chronic high control

RESOURCE TIP: For more information, read *Women Who*

Love Psychopaths: Inside the Relationships of Inevitable Harm with Psychopaths, Sociopaths, and Narcissists by Sandra Brown.

How to Know the Difference Between Toxic or Not Toxic

The biggest indicator of a toxic relationship is that there is a steady pattern of chaos. One way to recognize the difference between normal issues and issues that are more than just issues is to look for patterns over time. Since everyone makes mistakes and some mistakes are more hurtful than others, we can look at a person's behavior pattern over time to determine if there is toxicity in the relationship.

We can also look for the level of issues that arise. For example, if what comes up most often in the relationship is miscommunication, misunderstanding, or general confusion about something, these are things that happen in all relationships. If what comes up most often in the relationship is blatant disregard of your safety, your dignity, or cruel words or actions, that is a different level of toxic. How you feel needs to be okay in any relationship. While we may be susceptible to toxic relationships when we are in a vulnerable place in life, we stay in them because we ignore our intuition.

Three indicators of an unhealthy relationship are:

- contempt
- lack of empathy
- manipulation

Chances are if you are experiencing one of these in your

relationship over a period of time, the relationship has become unhealthy.

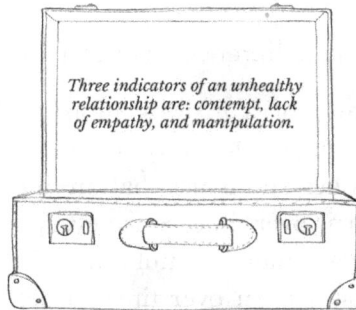

Three indicators of an unhealthy relationship are: contempt, lack of empathy, and manipulation.

Learning the warning signs

When we ignore our intuition, the best thing to do is to learn to trust ourselves again. When I was ready to begin dating again, I couldn't help but wonder: how can I make sure I never again become the victim of this type of damaging manipulation? Part of this trust building is to educate ourselves with our part in the relationships and to know and recognize the warning signs of toxic people.

Gaslighting

Gaslighting may be the most confusing, cruel tool in emotional manipulation. Here's how it works. Based on the 1944 movie *Gaslight*, the term refers to emotional manipulation tactics used to make one person feel like they're going crazy. Lexi was a skilled gaslighter, particularly when it came to other women.

Lexi and I had been dating about a year when Susan joined our book group. Susan and I became fast friends. One night,

Susan, Lexi, and I went out to a club and something felt off. It seemed like Susan and Lexi were flirting. I told myself I was being paranoid. Lexi later told me I was being insecure and reminded me of every bad relationship I'd had as a clue that whatever insecurity I felt was unjustified. At one point, Lexi and Susan went to the bar to get drinks and while I sat with other friends and chatted, something made me look their way. I realized Lexi was looking at Susan the way she used to look at me. I knew then that they would be together, whether she and I were broken up or not. I would find out later that I was exactly right. Still, as they met up after book club for drinks or texted nonstop, Lexi assured me they were just friends. Her response to me was to become righteously indignant and tell me I was insecure because of my "issues," and that I just didn't remember what it was like to be a good friend.

When I learned later that they were dating the last months of our relationship, I was more heartbroken by the betrayal of my new friend than I was over Lexi's gaslighting me about their relationship.

Intermittent Reinforcement

One of the most powerful manipulation tools used in toxic relationships is intermittent reinforcement. Life with Lexi was an addictive cycle of highs and lows that ate away at my sense of who I was to the point that I lost my confidence and boundaries in the relationship. I told myself that I stayed because I was in love. As life has it, things became crystal clear only after I moved out and moved on. One of my biggest aha moments came when my therapist introduced me to the concept of *intermittent reinforcement*. Scientists discovered the biological power of intermittent reinforcement in observing mice. In an experiment, mice pressed a lever and a morsel of food was delivered. In this consistent practice the mice eventually got full and stopped pressing the lever. Then researchers changed the pattern; sometimes when the lever was pressed food was delivered, sometimes it was not. The desired object (food) was intermittently reinforced. The mice not only pressed the lever obsessively, but they did so until they injured themselves from all the pressing. The fear of not receiving the reward was so strong they literally harmed themselves just for the chance of getting it.

When intermittent reinforcement is used in relationships, periods of love and affection are alternated with periods of abuse, neglect, and creating fear of losing the relationship. Fear is one of the biggest human motivators there is.

Many times, we have internal triggers that, when activated, latch onto another person. A powerful way to recognize intermittent reinforcement in your relationship is when there is a pattern of the other person pushing you away and pulling you back in. This happened for me in my relationship with Lexi. I also realized that I was engaging in unhealthy behaviors myself that kept me in the relationship far longer than was healthy for me.

Action Step: What You Can Do

Grab a journal and complete your own action step on making a plan to identify toxic relationships sooner.

1. Go back to your earlier exercise from this chapter and note the words you wrote in the margin.
2. Jot down some of those words (e.g., denying your reality, demeaning), leaving some space underneath each.
3. Underneath each word or phrase write a state in the positive that is an example of the opposite of that behavior. For example, for denying your reality, I would write "Can hear and care about my viewpoint, accepts responsibility."

4. Continue this pattern until you have 4-5 statements.
5. Rewrite your statements as sentences that begin with "I will look for." For example, here are some of mine:

- (Intermittent reinforcement) I will look for consistency. The best way to know someone is to observe them over time. Predictability is the opposite of intermittent reinforcement.
- (Raging, general chaos) I will look for signs of a healthy relationship like trust, shared values, respect, intimacy, and commitment. Fear, drama, imbalance, and never knowing what's going to happen are <u>not</u> love. Manipulation, contempt, and lack of empathy are signs of an unhealthy relationship.
- (Denying your reality) I will look for the capacity to hear and care about my viewpoint and accept responsibility.

In order to learn to trust myself again, I had to unravel the ways that I talked myself into staying in that relationship. I began by asking myself: what were the details of the timing? What did you see in her? Why did you choose to start dating her? Why when I began to see examples of toxic behaviors did I choose to say? How did I abandon myself in the relationship?

Learning to trust ourselves again

Regardless of the other person's issues, when we identify our own role in relationships, we are practicing self-responsibility. For example, even in my most toxic relationship with Lexi I learned many things about myself. I learned what my triggers are and how I get compelled into unhealthy patterns. I learned that in the face of aggression, and criticism, I freeze and become passive. This freezing is my responsibility and is something that I continue to work on.

It is not our job to fix someone else. Most people are doing the best they can and we're all on our own journey. Someone with toxic behavior patterns is unfixable until they themselves decide to get help. The other thing about toxic relationship patterns is that they're not personal. While we know this person is not behaving this way because of us, it doesn't mean that it needs to happen on our watch. It doesn't mean that we have to take responsibility for repairing the damage done to the other person. Only they can do that. In order to grow in intimacy and connection in all human relationships, we all need the capacity and willingness to grow.

Summary

We are ultimately responsible for everything that happens in our lives. We also don't live in a vacuum and every once in a while, we may get into a relationship with someone who has more than just issues. This happens when we ignore our intuition and are vulnerable because of past trauma, grief, or stress. When we gain the ability to recognize our part in getting in and staying in toxic relationships and apply tools to identify them sooner, we are more empowered and less prone to being abused. We are not here to be abused. Learning to trust ourselves once we have been in a toxic relationship is key to knowing and recognizing the warning signs sooner. When we get healthier we attract healthier.

Section 3: Inspiring Our Future

6

Empowering Ourselves

The hardest thing about change is making a different choice than the day before. The moment you don't feel whatever emotion you've felt over and over, you don't know who you are.—*Joe DiSpenza*

As women, we often get into relationships, even healthy ones, and lose ourselves. We are conditioned to be caregivers and abandon ourselves, our own needs, hobbies, and friends. This model is not only unsustainable, but it actually can become the reason for the demise of our relationship. Self-abandonment is the number one relationship killer.

We abandon our own needs

In order to understand my pattern of abandoning my own needs in relationships, I had to untangle how I got there in the first place.

I have spent my entire life trying to blend in, trying not to be the center of attention. As a kid, we moved a lot, sometimes every school year. I became an expert at feeling out the situation, quietly blending into the background, making my presence easy to overlook. I would endure the embarrassing introduction to the class, then sit in the back and decide who the nice kids were, who the ones to avoid were, and who I could trust to sit by me at lunch without pity.

Our human instincts kick in when we experience chaos. Our biological conditioning for survival—freeze, flight, or fight—predisposes us to habits that may help us survive chaos, but don't necessarily serve us in the rest of our lives. For me, freeze was my go-to response during chaos. Much like a wild animal that simply hides, I found myself observing carefully from the sidelines. I became highly skilled at taking in every piece of information available in any situation, like tone of voice, body language, facial expressions, and actions or lack of actions that said, "You don't belong here. You are invisible".

In dating and relationships, I played small. I became like a superhero at taking care of myself when I was single. But then I'd get in a relationship and bam! It was like I switched capes from superhero to myself to super-codependent to someone else. Over time, I lost my voice in the relationship and eventually my place as a valued partner. I repeated this pattern over and over where bold, strong Kim would deteriorate slowly, without awareness into small, silent Kim, the one who nothing can ever be about, until eventually even big things couldn't be about me —birthdays, relative's funerals, job losses and promotions, even serious illness.

The frog in the water metaphor

The frog in boiling water metaphor explains why we get trapped in these unhealthy dynamics. The fable goes that if a frog jumps into hot water it will immediately jump out. But if it jumps in a pan of lukewarm water and the water is slowly heated, the frog won't perceive the danger and it will die. Similarly, none of us would put up with being ignored, minimized, disrespected, or disregarded when we first start dating someone. But when it happens gradually over time, in ways we may be so unaware of, by the time we can no longer ignore it we are in a dangerously hot pot of water with no clear path out. One reason we abandon our own needs is because we are conditioned to be caregivers. This can make us ill prepared to step into our own power in being our authentic, whole selves.

Increasing our self-care

One of the best tools in countering self-abandonment is to increase our self-care. So how do we find our way back to ourselves when we got lost in a relationship? Or better yet, how do we hang on to ourselves confidently enough to not get lost in the first place? Like all things in life, the path to the answers begins with asking ourselves more empowering questions. When difficult things happen, we often ask ourselves disempowering questions like:

- Why is this happening to me?
- Why me?

We can shift to more empowering questions like:

- What am I learning from this?
- What is unfolding in my life right now?
- How can I love myself through this?
- What do I need right now?

In dating and relationships, rather than asking, "Why is she totally ignoring my needs?" we can ask ourselves, "In what ways am I ignoring my own needs?" By focusing our attention on the role we are playing in our own suffering, we raise our awareness to what is happening in each moment and empower ourselves to be our own solution, rather than giving away our power to someone or something else.

Soul Truth

SELF-ABANDONMENT

---

is the

No. 1

relationship

killer

My rock bottom

My own practice in shifting to more empowering questions began when I hit rock bottom, physically. After my hysterectomy, I spent two years trying to get back to who I was before I got sick. My iron and hemoglobin numbers came up. But everything else seemed to be out of whack. My blood sugar was off, making me hungry all the time and frequently shaky. My thyroid and hormones were off, which led to weight gain no matter how much I worked out. I began seeing a naturopath and taking supplements for my blood sugar, thyroid, hormones, and other vitamin deficiencies. All the while I kept trying to get back to running as it was my main form of stress relief and exercise prior to my surgery.

If I could just run again

I kept telling myself that if I could just run again, without pain, then I would be me again and I committed to running another half marathon. I was cranking along in my training, when, after a hard hill run, I woke up the next morning with a pulled hip. I went to the sports chiropractor who always got me well and ready for the start line. But I noticed something different this time. All my joints hurt. Some days it felt like I had the flu, everything ached so much. I went to therapy at the chiropractor and would get a little relief, but by the next morning my hip would be aching again, along with everything from my right middle toe to my finger joints. Still I kept on, determined that if I could finish a half marathon again I would be back to me.

Shortly before race weekend, I visited my family in the Midwest. I spent the day chasing my young nephew all over the park, laughing, and playing. I was in heaven. He was three, and a bundle of energy. When I woke up the next day, I felt like I had been hit by a truck. At first, I thought I was just sore from lifting him in ways that I maybe hadn't been lifting things.

But as my Monday workday went on, I felt worse and worse. Over my lunch break I got a deep tissue massage hoping that it would help relieve the pain. I took ibuprofen and kept the heating pad on my neck and back. Nothing seemed to help. I pushed my way through my workday and wondered if maybe I did actually have the flu. Deeply frustrated and exhausted from being in pain, I flew home the next day determined to do whatever I had to do to get well.

Luckily, I felt a little bit better each day the following week and was able to slowly get back to running. I completed my training and ran a half marathon at about the same pace I have run every half marathon. But something felt different. Everything began to hurt around mile five. Instead of feeling my legs getting looser and the run getting easier, it got harder. It felt like I had never run before. My legs and joints hurt. As a runner, sometimes you just don't have a good run. I decided that this day was one of those runs. I put on my headphones and told myself something I had been wearing on my shirt: *Nevertheless she persisted*. And I did. I crossed the finish line. But my accomplishment was paired with searing pain in my back and hips, and a darkening sense that something was really wrong with me.

━━━

I committed to recovering from the race slowly. Because everything hurt, I couldn't lift weights or do any other kind of exercise. I had a lingering toe pain that was so bad I couldn't wear shoes. I switched my exercise habit to yoga. I began eating grain-free. Within 48 hours of removing all grain from my diet, the inflammation in my joints subsided, and the pain I had been experiencing was significantly reduced. I lost a few pounds, and the brain fog I had been struggling with post-surgery finally began to lift.

As I explained my symptoms to my doctor, along with the recent relief from eating grain-free, she suggested that it was possible that I had Lyme disease. Lyme disease is caused by the bacterium *Borrelia burgdorferi* and is transmitted to humans through the bite of an infected tick.

I initially blew her off and when the test came back negative felt like I was right. But as she explained that about half of Lyme testing isn't accurate because of limitations in the labs and the types of bacteria each test examines, it occurred to me that every single one of my symptoms was consistent with Lyme. Everything else that it could be had been ruled out. My eyes welled up with tears when I realized I would have to accept that I was experiencing the symptoms of something that was permanent, complicated, and that maybe meant I could never run again.

For the next week I grieved and got really mad. First, I was mad at my doctors for not recognizing the signs sooner. Then I was mad at Western medicine for having shitty tests that don't diagnose accurately. Then I was mad at myself for possibly contracting the disease. When I was done being mad, and grieving in general about being sick, I began asking myself more empowering questions. The same is true in relationships. When something happens that feels out of our control or unjust, like when we have a fight or feel unheard in some way, we can begin to take our power back in the situation by changing the questions we ask ourselves.

----

*I still don't know for certain if I have Lyme
disease or not. In the end, it doesn't really
matter to me anyway. These days I focus on
treating the symptoms and supporting my
immune system in its entirety.*

Action Step: What You Can Do

Grab a journal and complete your own action step on asking
yourself more empowering questions.

1. Jot down a situation in your life that is bothering you.
2. Write down as many thoughts and feelings you have
   about the situation that come to you. Let your words
   flow freely, try not to judge them.
3. See if you can identify what about the situation feels
   unfair, unjust, or that makes you feel like a victim.
4. Thinking back to the thoughts-become-reality
   exercise in chapter three, what are some empowering
   questions you can ask yourself about this situation?
   For example, when my body started falling apart, I
   was asking myself "How did I ever get in this
   situation?", which is another flavor for "Why me?" I
   tried switching to "What am I learning from this
   situation right now in this moment?"

▭

Note: Identifying empowering questions for ourselves in times
of difficulty does NOT remove responsibility from people who

are being abusive. Nor does it excuse or make right things that are indeed unjust. The purpose of the empowering question is that it allows us to pivot back to what we can control: how we react.

Healing

Around this time, one of my health practitioners recommended a couple of self-care techniques, and a book that would eventually change everything for me, *How to Heal Yourself When No One Else Can* (2016). In the book, author Amy Scher, who suffered from severe symptoms of Lyme disease for years, shares her journey and ultimate discovery that many of her symptoms came down to emotional causes. As a die-hard science-based person, I rolled my eyes at the idea of the connection between emotions and body systems malfunctioning. Could it really be that simple? But at this point in my life I was so discouraged, I would have done anything to feel better. I was unwilling to accept life as a sedentary person, being constantly in pain, with an identity wrapped around being sick. If eating grain-free meant my joints didn't hurt as much, I would be grain-free forever. If doing yoga instead of running meant my body didn't ache constantly and I didn't need physical therapy to be able to sit up straight, then that's what I would do. From this book and from this phase of my life came the best lesson I have ever learned up to this point.

> ***I learned that abandoning my own needs is the very thing that was making me sicker.***

This is in line with the soul truth I talked about earlier that what we resist persists. In fact, the only thing that had ever stopped me from continuing in toxic situations, including relationships, a toxic job, and engaging in activities that were harming my body in its current condition, was literally losing the physical ability to continue. Having the habit of pushing through pain and ignoring my body's warning signs was the highest form of self-abandonment and I had been doing it for years. During this phase, I began to view things differently.

———

RESOURCE TIP: For more information about Lyme disease, read *How Can I Get Better?: An Action Plan for Treating Resistant Lyme & Chronic Disease* by Richard Horowitz.

RESOURCE TIP: For more information about healing physically and emotionally, read *How to Heal Yourself When No One Else Can: A Total Self-Healing Approach for Mind, Body, and Spirit* by Amy Scher.

———

Identify what does and doesn't serve you

How does all this relate to dating and relationships? Earlier I mentioned that self-abandonment is the number one relationship killer. We can't build healthy relationships until we have a consistent pattern of taking care of ourselves. Building the habit of identifying what is healthy to us is a powerful tool. For me, this works by examining what serves me in my life's purpose and what does not. For example, I have had a habit of being a more available friend in some of my friendships than my friends were available to me. Then at one of life's lowest moments when I lost sight of who I was and was living in new city 500 miles away from home, up to my neck in schoolwork and stress, I needed my friends more than ever. But they weren't available. Because I had the habit of pushing my needs and feelings away, I didn't reach out to them or ask for help.

Building the habit of identifying what is healthy to us is a powerful tool.

What I realized about some of those friendships is that I had never established a place in the relationship. I was the fun one, the one who could be counted on to organize a party or an event, and who would listen when others were suffering. I had never established a presence as a vulnerable, authentic person who needed support once in a while. I also didn't have the language to express vulnerability or ask for help. At the very worst possible time, much like being sick with Lindsay as my support, I realized that what I most needed was not available to me. Later, as I began to get back on my feet and reestablish myself, I realized that those friendships, while they served a purpose in my life for a timeframe, no longer served me. Those dynamics did not serve me, and I chose to let them go.

Action Step: What You Can Do

Grab a journal and complete your own action step on identifying things that serve you.

1. Review your notes from previous action steps, particularly on recovering from grief.
2. See if you can identify some behaviors or activities that lift you up when you feel spun out. Here are a few of mine: running, singing, listening to music, reading in a quiet place, taking a walk, connecting with a friend for dinner, on the phone, or on FaceTime, and creative journaling.
3. Choose one of the activities you listed and engage in it for 15-30 minutes before moving on to number 4.
4. Now that you are more grounded you can find a quiet place, take a few deep breaths, and reflect. Consider your life as it is right now, on any given day, any given week, and ask yourself the following questions:

- What in my day to day activities feels lined up with who I am? (For example, whenever I am collaborating with colleagues I feel completely in line with my strengths and values.)
- What do I do that feels empowering and makes me feel like my best self, or is confidence boosting? (For example, when I speak up for myself, whether it's asserting my feelings or asking for what I want, I feel nervous at first, but then I feel a surge of self-confidence that I can take care of myself).
- Continue finding examples of the questions, listing as many words that fit you as possible. (For example, some of mine are: collaborating, speaking my truth, sitting in quiet, and being engaged in tasks in the present moment).

These are the things that serve you. It may be helpful to make a goal to do more of them throughout your day or week.

The role of self-judgment

For me, my pushing on versus listening to my body came down to a belief I had about resting. At some point, my way of coping became to stay really busy and to keep a lot of balls in the air in my life. The strategy worked really well when I was in college and working, or when I was teaching full-time and going to graduate school full-time, or when I wanted to be a really good teacher and had to work long days and weekends and holidays to learn how. Where this wasn't serving me any longer was in taking care of my body and my heart. I was full of self-judgment about my body and not being able to run. My self-judgment was reflected in perfectionism that I held as an expectation for myself.

How to do things that feed you

Doing things that feed you is good for the soul. For example, music, art, and creativity can be incredibly fulfilling to balance out our daily responsibilities in life.

One of the most powerful ways to find our way back to ourselves is by dialing in to the body. This means, in times of stress, rather than detaching from our suffering through drinking, staying really busy, complaining, spending money, or other unhealthy habits, we turn instead toward ourselves. What this looks like is often just a quiet asking of ourselves, "What is happening right now? I am feeling a lot of anger and a strong desire to run away." If we can be with our feelings, allowing them to come on fully rather than escaping them, we can actually use them to align our thoughts and actions. Feelings are not wrong, they are trying to tell us something. When we tune in to them and respond accordingly, we are practicing good self-care and standing in our own power.

We are social creatures and aren't meant to do everything alone or to be alone all the time. Yet in a culture that demonizes needing things or vulnerability, and reveres independence and success, it is easy to get caught up in connecting technologically rather than in person. Self-care is loving what is, and being okay with ourselves. It all comes down to us. We can either empower or disempower ourselves.

Another important piece to acknowledge is to catch ourselves when we get stuck. Sometimes we get into a rut and don't realize our self-care has slipped. In the spirit of avoiding perfectionism, the important thing is not to make sure that never happens, but to catch ourselves when it does. One tool is to practice awareness-raising behaviors, such as meditation, checking in with the body, and physical activity that serves you.

> *Self-care is loving what is, and being okay with ourselves. It all comes down to us. We can either empower or disempower ourselves.*

Summary

Practicing self-care isn't about living in a bubble or sweeping things under the rug, it's about pivoting from abandoning our own needs to increasing our self-empowerment in our lives. We often abandon ourselves because we are conditioned as women to be caregivers or we are ill prepared to step into our full power in being whole just as we are. Self-abandonment is the number one relationship killer, and improving our self-care can take our relationships to a whole new level.

7

Practicing Healthy Habits

We become what we repeatedly do.—Sean Covey

One of the key aspects in taking care of ourselves in relationships is practicing healthy habits. Practicing healthy habits keeps us from abandoning ourselves in the first place.

Developing unhealthy habits

When we get into a relationship, it is easy to develop unhealthy habits or lose sight of healthy ones. We stop working out, seeing our friends or family, or doing things we love.

One of the reasons we develop unhealthy habits, or fail to practice healthy ones, as we focus on the relationship is for the same reasons all our other challenges happen. We are habitually unconscious. We fall into victim thinking. We're conditioned to ignore our feelings. We lose alignment with ourselves. We revert to the familiar. We doubt our worth, and we're conditioned to be caregivers.

One of the most powerful tools in developing healthier habits in thoughts and daily routines is to acknowledge what is not working for us, course-correct, and establish habits and routines that do serve us.

Coping with stress

Habits like sleep, maintaining our support systems, eating healthy and regularly, moving our bodies, engaging in hobbies, and managing our finances are all part of living a full life.

Healthy coping strategies include:

- how to calm ourselves down when we get triggered or activated
- how to self soothe
- how to communicate our needs and feelings
- how to stand in the truth of who we are consistently

When it comes to healthy habits, consistency is key. Things like meditating, practicing gratitude, keeping a daily routine, and engaging in stress-relieving activities like exercising are keys to practicing healthy habits.

Another habit is to develop tools for soothing ourselves when we get worked up or triggered. Some of the following are common ones that I have learned and that have helped me stay healthy and relate directly to taking care of myself in relationships.

Tapping

Tapping, or emotional freedom technique (EFT), is a tool used to soothe the nervous system when we get triggered and to release unresolved emotional issues. The idea is that emotions get stuck in the body and cause blockages in our energy systems. Tapping is a process that removes the blockages. There are several main tapping points:

- The top of the head
- Eyebrow
- Side of the eye
- Under the eye
- Under the nose
- Chin
- Collarbone
- Under the arm/side of the body

Practitioners vary in their approach to tapping. Generally, the practice involves rating the intensity of the experience you're having, tapping through the tapping points on your body, and checking in to see how the intensity has changed. For example, if my partner and I have an argument, the kind that keeps resurfacing because it's an old painful issue, my body is likely in a stress state. To soothe it and help me process my intense emotions, I will find a quiet place and begin telling the situation out loud as if I'm talking to a friend. I don't hold back; I express all the concrete details including my feelings, sights, smells, and sounds. While I am telling the story, I begin gently tapping through the tapping points, using two fingers gently. The following example illustrates the process I use from beginning to end.

After finding a quiet place and taking a few deep breaths, I think about the triggering event that is causing stress to feel stuck in my body. In this example, my partner didn't tell me that her ex-girlfriend was going to be at a party we attended. It had been an ongoing issue as there were some poor boundaries with the ex at the beginning of our relationship. I check in with my body and rate the intensity of my stress around this issue an eight. Then I begin to tap and tell the story aloud.

- *Top of the head*—I can't believe she didn't tell me her ex was going to be at the party.
- *Eyebrow*—I remember all the other times she kept secrets about her ex.
- *Side of the eye*—I remember the last conversation we had about her ex and she acknowledged her ex is still into her and promised to have better boundaries with her.
- *Under the eye*—I remember the first time I felt like my boundaries were violated.
- *Under the nose*—I felt foolish and like I was being played.
- *Chin*—I feel small and foolish and wonder if I'm being insecure of if anyone would feel this way?
- *Collarbone*—My stomach is jittery, and my heart feels like it's sinking into my chest.
- *Under the arm*—Why the hell keep secrets if it's no big deal?

I would then take a deep breath and check in with my body to see how the intensity rates. If it's still a seven or eight, I'd continue tapping, starting at the top of my head again, going through all the tapping points and talking out loud.

Some practitioners offer a more structured approach that involves setting up a statement and some other components. For me, I find that just talking through intense emotions while tapping is incredibly comforting.

The goal in tapping is to calm the nervous system, soothe ourselves, and release old stuck energy. Because the goal isn't to find a solution or push away our feelings, tapping can be a powerful self-care technique.

RESOURCE TIP: For more information about tapping, read *The Tapping Solution: A Revolutionary System for Stress-Free Living* by Nick Ortner.

Releasing

Another impact on the body in times of stress is the buildup of stress hormones. Releasing the intense emotions using a physical motion can clear out the flight or fight chemicals and help your body return to a calmer state. While thinking about the triggering event:

- Press as hard as you can against a wall (leaning on it, not rapid pushing or punching)
- Yell into a pillow (or your arm when you're not at home)
- Bounce a ball really hard against the pavement

The goal is to give your body an outlet for the initial buildup of stress chemicals so they don't get stuck in your body. It's about self-care, not justifying losing your shit. Key components of these releasing techniques are that you are alone in a safe place, and that the releasing technique doesn't harm you or anyone else.

The goal is to give your body an outlet for the stress chemicals that build up so they don't get stuck in your body.

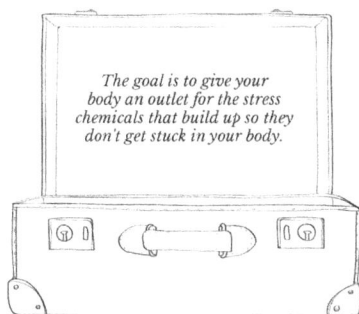

Managing our thoughts

Another healthy habit is to practice gratitude and to set our intentions at the beginning of the day before we get caught up in schedules and social media and what is most pressing to us that day. This habit has really helped me focus on how I want to feel instead of letting life happen and then just reacting to it. In addition, being mindful or present in the moment is a wonderfully healthy habit. For me this mostly means meditating daily, even if it's only for five minutes at a time. It also means dialing in to the warning signs that I am fluttering above my own life and not very present in the moment. For me, warning signs that I need to get grounded are:

- feeling extremely distracted
- having a hard time being present and listening to people
- feeling shaky or anxious
- having a hard time sleeping
- having a hard time enjoying each moment
- losing interest in things that I normally find enjoyable
- losing my train of thought frequently

Practicing gratitude is another daily habit that helps keep us grounded and reinforces the law of attraction. Creating a grounded morning practice can help focus our thoughts on what we do want rather than what we don't want, which ultimately attracts more.

Action Step: What You Can Do

Grab a journal and complete your own action step of creating a morning routine.

1. Think back to your earlier action step and list of things that serve you.
2. See if you can identify those that help you feel grounded, calm, and present.
3. Start a new list that includes ideas for a morning self-care practice. Include habits you have now or have used in the past, activities friends or loved ones have in the mornings, or borrow some from books. (Hal Elrod's book below is an excellent source).

Here is my morning routine:

- Coffee and meditate for 10 minutes
- Set 2-3 intentions for the day (I try to include at least 1 feeling or thought, e.g., I want to feel grateful, supported, and to contribute).
- List 4-5 things I feel grateful for

Set your alarm for 30-45 minutes earlier in the morning and try out your routine for a week. It took me a few weeks to feel a difference in how I felt throughout my day.

———

RESOURCE TIP: For more information about morning routines, read *Miracle Mornings for Writers: How to Build a Writing Ritual That Increases Your Impact and Your Income* by Hal Elrod and Steve Scott.

———

Another key healthy habit for me that has been life-changing is establishing healthy boundaries with my life. I realized that my tendency is to be afraid of missing out, which often leads me to overcommitting, or overplanning my week. This overplanning leads to very little still time, which is when I rejuvenate and dial the most in to how I'm feeling. My boundaries are now about balancing social and alone time, balancing time with my friends and my partner, and sometimes just giving myself permission to stay home and be really boring. The important thing here isn't that we set and follow our boundaries and follow healthy habits perfectly, but that we recalibrate, and course-correct when we get off course. Part of developing healthier habits is to identify unhealthy habits in relationships.

Soul Truth

We
empower
ourselves

by practicing
HEALTHY HABITS
daily

Unhealthy relationship habits

In one moment, I knew. After many years, moves, job changes, and a brief stint in couple's therapy, we were in the middle of yet another argument. I don't remember what it was about, but I remember feeling like we were speaking different languages. Confused, I finally I blurted, "Do you even care about how I feel?" Quite matter-of-factly, Lindsay answered, "Why should I have to worry about how you feel?" And I knew. It all made sense. In that moment she literally told me she didn't value me or my feelings anymore. There was nothing left to do but to begin the long process of untangling our complicated relationship.

Later, after I began to put Humpty back together again, I wondered: why is it that when it comes to relationships, we often hang on tighter even when evidence shows that there's just nothing left for us there? Since all relationships bring up issues, how do we know the difference between normal stuff and when a relationship just isn't working? I realized that sometimes it was fear of failure that caused me to stay put or I got stuck in the details. We were living together or had paid for a vacation. Mostly, I stayed too long in relationships because I just didn't know how to know it was over.

After 20 years of staying too long at the party, I identified four patterns that help me recognize when a relationship has unhealthy habits and it's time to move on.

Four ways to know it's time to move on

1. You're hanging in for nostalgia

It is so confusing, when remembering the good times from early on, to accept that things have changed. I have had the tendency when it comes to love to resist change, to ignore it, and metaphorically stomp my feet in pouty protest. Over time, I discovered that once I am just holding on hoping it will be the way it once was, or that things will change in the ways I need in order for the relationship to work for me, it is over.

2. You have lost things

In chapter five, I talked about how love shouldn't hurt. Or cause you to lose things like sleep, friends, or focus on goals. This has been such a hard thing for me to accept because all relationships take some work. What I understand now is that the line is loss. Once a pattern develops that involves me losing things—a sense of me, health, etc.—the relationship has deteriorated into an unhealthy one and it's time to cut my losses.

3. She is stuck and unwilling to grow

Taking responsibility for ourselves takes courage and the ability to tolerate our own limitations. Whether due to a personality disorder, untreated addiction, or general immaturity, some people, at certain points in their lives, lack the capacity for taking responsibility. You can spot this in someone when you notice she will not say I'm sorry, or when she does something shitty and then blames it on you. Or there is a chronic lack of awareness of how her behavior impacts you. No matter how much you may love a person, you really can't work with a blamer who is unwilling to take responsibility for herself.

4. She broke a deal breaker

Deal breakers are the boundaries you set before you're in love that say what you will and won't put up with in relationships. Aside from the biggies like cheating, there are many others like shutting down during conflict, punishing behaviors when a wrong is perceived, or financial instability. Looking back, it's clear to me that once a deal breaker was cracked for either of us in the relationship, it was a turning point—one that should have indicated it was time to end it.

Maybe we stay too long in relationships because we're in love, or because of perceived failures. I realized all of the patterns come down to one thing, the solution for what to do lies in the answer to one question: Am I compromising who I am?

Prevention techniques

How do we keep ourselves from getting lost in the first place? The chapters leading up to this one, particularly the chapter on healing the past, are good foundations for holding ourselves valuable in relationships. In addition, it helps to have a sense of humor about ourselves. One thing that I have noticed in myself as I have aged is a tendency for my judgment to come out more and more. What I know now about judgment is the more that I am judging others, the more it stems from my own self-judgment. Self-judgment does not serve us. It does not make us better at the things that we do nor motivate us to become our best selves. Instead it leads to what I call, "Get off my lawn you kids!" behaviors like couples who never go out and criticize anyone who does. Or the couple that has eye rolling, inside joke glances, and general judgment for just about anyone that isn't them. What has happened in these situations is that over time the only thing these couples have in common with each other is their ability to judge other people. Tara Brach talks about judgment as a tool for coping with our own sense of unworthiness. In *Meditations for Emotional Healing*, she describes judgment as keeping us locked in a sense of deficiencies and we blame others. I began to notice this and myself the year that I struggled with my health. I was coming home from a dinner out, a dinner I am fortunate enough to be able to afford, a dinner I was looking forward to because I got to wear my fancy heels and my red lipstick, which I rarely did anymore. I was looking forward to it because I got alone time with one of my favorite people. Still, on the drive home I heard myself complaining about the service, about the food, and it hit me: I was one step away from yelling at kids to get off my lawn. These days I watch for judgment, and I know that when I'm judging others, it is just a reflection for how I'm judging myself. Sometimes I will even say out loud, "Get off my lawn!" to shake me out of my own cycle.

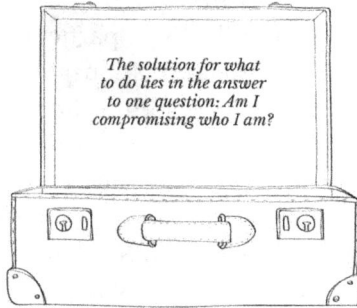

The solution for what to do lies in the answer to one question: Am I compromising who I am?

My biggest loss

I have experienced a lot of loss in life. But the biggest loss I have ever experienced was losing my integrity. I had been dating Cali in a long-distance relationship. We were ultimately probably not very compatible. But I really loved her, and at the time I didn't know what to do. So, I did what I always did up to that point—I buried my feelings. We broke up and got back together a few times. The same incompatibility issues always emerged again. However, the last time, since I was in try-harder mode, and had other stressors in my life, my way of dealing with my sadness over our ultimate incompatibility was to ignore it. This worked for a little while. It all came to a horrible intersection one night when I went out with friends. My best friend at the time, Misty, and I had become more flirtatious over time. Because I was ignoring the stressors in my life, ignoring the problems in my relationship with Cali, and ignoring most of my feelings in general, it was easy to ignore the developing flirtation with Misty. I chalked it up to innocent flirting with a friend. Even writing that now it's hard to believe I ever convinced myself of those words. But there it is, and there I was. So, I ignored my feelings when they came up, did not communicate my feelings and my fears, and instead focused on my friends. I would come home at the end of a night out and call Cali and talk about how grateful we were to have each other. I was full of judgment for all the other single women out there. They didn't have what I had, I told myself. Meanwhile, in real life, what was really brewing inside me was a general unease with my relationship, and a deep knowing that being with her not only made me feel like I wasn't being myself, but that I lost a piece of me.

After a night of drinking and partying and inevitable flirting, Misty kissed me. And I kissed her back. We ended up sleeping together that night. In that moment, I not only betrayed Cali, but I betrayed the most important person of all that I should have integrity with—myself.

The story did not end here and did not play out well for anyone. What I learned many months later, is that I became in a toxic relationship with myself the moment I decided to ignore my feelings. In each moment I chose to shove away my feelings, whether it was about Cali and I being incompatible, or about getting some connection needs met by my friend Misty, no matter how inappropriate, all that ignoring developed into a toxic relationship with myself. The other thing I had to do to move forward from that situation was that I had to learn to forgive myself. Ultimately, I came clean with Cali, and decided to take responsibility for cheating on her.

Acknowledging my role

I would like to stop the story here and say that I did what I thought was the right thing and called Cali the next morning to tell her what I did and allowed her some dignity in this situation. However, to further display just how far I was from myself, I did call her and break up with her, I just didn't tell her the full truth. I told myself at the time I didn't tell her about the cheating because why hurt her? I was doing it for her. I was being a nice person. In that moment I really believed the lie I told myself. Fast-forward two years, and as I was getting out of and abusive, toxic relationship with Lexi, I realized it all began with cheating on Cali. That's when I originally got lost. Then I was so disgusted with who I was that I decided no one would want to date a cheater. I allowed emotional abuse and manipulation to happen in my life as a sort of self-punishment. The worst thing I ever did to someone else was cheat. The worst thing I ever did to myself was to lose sight of who I am and trade my integrity for avoidance.

How to know when we get lost

The number one question that we can ask ourselves to check in on if our soul gets lost in a situation is: *do I feel stuck, trapped, disengaged, or unhappy*? Another sign can be rigid thinking, or an underlying feeling of restlessness. One warning here, in our culture, it is tempting to place blame on other people. It can be tempting, when we are suffering, to blame our relationship, and to have this fairytale mindset that if only I was single, or if only my partner was _____, or if only I was with someone else, everything would be great. What I have learned after 20 years of dating is that when I am suffering and trapped, it is because I have abandoned myself. No matter what relationship I am in at the time, coming back to me has to happen first before I can untangle if something in the relationship needs to be addressed.

One of the ways that we avoid self-abandonment is to catch ourselves when we fall into the habit of losing ourselves sooner. For example, if we can identify the ways that we have lost ourselves in relationships in the past, we can put virtual safeguards in place so that we catch ourselves if we start to fall into the same pattern later. Identifying the ways we sabotage ourselves is one step.

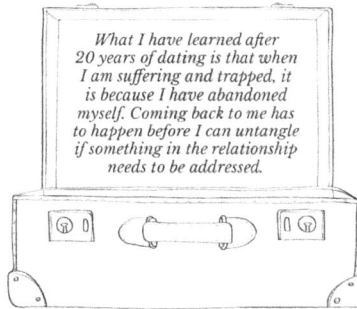

What I have learned after 20 years of dating is that when I am suffering and trapped, it is because I have abandoned myself. Coming back to me has to happen before I can untangle if something in the relationship needs to be addressed.

Self-sabotage

Sometimes when we have false beliefs about ourselves, like I'm not good enough, we create self-fulfilling prophecies in our lives. For example, part of my "I'm invisible" belief is the feeling that I just don't matter that much to people. This belief is so old and so deep, I'm often not even aware that I am carrying it around and acting on it. My I'm invisible belief showed up so clearly in a situation with my sister-in-law. I was visiting a friend in a city near where my brother and sister-in-law live one weekend. It didn't even occur to me to contact them to meet up. First, I was unaware of just how close the cities were. I had flown across the country and so I wasn't very present to where I was in relationship to where they lived. Also, it was during the time when my health was floundering, and I was at rock bottom with debilitating cramps and severe anemia. Those were real conditions of the situation. But the underlying condition that wasn't obvious to me was what I told myself at the time. *They* (my brother and sister-in-law) *aren't going to want to spend time with me—why would they want that? No one really cares when I'm around.* So, I operated on these beliefs without even being aware I was doing it and didn't contact my family. When my sister-in-law found out we were close by and didn't contact her or my brother, her feelings were deeply hurt. She felt like we didn't prioritize them, and she was right. Later, as I listened to her share her perspective, it occurred to me that because I minimized myself in the situation, I inadvertently made my brother and his wife feel unimportant! The irony was almost too much. I simply couldn't imagine that they valued and loved me enough to want to spend time with me, even though I had plenty of evidence that they did. This moment was a real wake-up call for me and I couldn't help but wonder how many other times my belief that I don't matter to people actually ended up hurting someone else.

The same accidental self-sabotage can happen in dating and relationships. For example, if I'm operating in my I-don't-matter belief, I won't text or reach out to a girl I'm interested in very much. Why would she want to hear from me? She's busy working. I don't want to come across as clingy. Inevitably, what happens? She thinks I'm not into her! Why wouldn't she? Just like my sister-in-law story, my own limiting beliefs about myself actually sabotaged my connection with the very person who was trying to have a relationship with me.

What to do when we get lost

When we realize that we are lost, what can we do about it? Turning our attention to re-prioritizing ourselves is a great place to start. For me, this always begins by recognizing that I am stuck in an obsessive thinking pattern, usually about another person's behavior or actions.

One really great technique to re-prioritize is to think back to what life was like before you got lost in the first place. Be careful; this isn't about where you were living, where you were working, who you were with, or how skinny you were. It may seem like that on the outside, but it is actually about our thinking, our habits, our self-care, and how empowered we felt in our lives. Seeing if we can identify what was going on in the timeframe that we began to lose ourselves can help us untangle the internal mess and find a roadmap back to ourselves. I had to do this with my cheating situation, and I could only do it after enough time passed and I had flogged myself with punishment for long enough.

The great news is re-prioritizing yourself does not have to equal blowing up our lives, breaking up, moving to a new state, or getting a new job. Re-prioritizing is simply a change in our own mindset and habits. Sometimes when we re-prioritize, we realize we need to make changes that are sometimes inevitable. But I strongly encourage anyone who is considering re-prioritizing to do so for themselves first before making any major external changes. This will allow you time to gain confidence in your decisions and give yourself space to fully realize whatever is happening in the moment.

Self-care also plays out in our attitude. When we are practicing regular self-care we generally maintain an attitude of hope, optimism, gratitude, and feel engaged in life.

> *For this reason, protecting our self-care habits with our lives needs to be number one priority.*

Healthy Relationship Habits

How to handle conflict

Recently, I stood in my backyard, hands on my hips, watching the steady demolition of my 80-year-old garage. As the whole thing came down and eventually became piles of splintered wood, it occurred to me that maybe tearing down a structure in order to build it back up is the best metaphor of all when it comes to relationships. At the beginning of a relationship, everyone is on polite mode. We show our best sides, and when things come up, we let them roll off our backs. Because we're in love. Because we're just learning about each other. Over time, as the relationship evolves, there comes a point when shit gets real—a genuine conflict emerges and in order to continue in intimacy, something needs a little tearing down, so it can be built back up. It's all about how we handle it. There are a few upsides to conflict.

Benefits of conflict

It's an opportunity for closeness

Unless you're fortunate enough to grow up in the unicorn 100% highly functioning family, chances are there are some gaps in your communication skills. For me, it has taken most of my adult life to learn how to identify and communicate my needs and feelings in relationships. The best thing about a relationship bump is that it is the opportunity to get everything out on the table. Without open, honest, vulnerable communication, true intimacy isn't possible. The good news is that working through conflict in an open way not only gets things out on the table, it actually brings you closer.

It's an opportunity to get to know each other better

Conflict and how we talk about it allows us to get to know

each other and ourselves better. Conflict lets you see her character. Does she need a little space after conflict? Does she fly off the handle and get mean? Does humor help stabilize the situation? What about a shared activity? These are important details to know when deciding if she's the one for you. Conflict also creates the opportunity to stay dialed in to our own needs.

It is an opportunity to practice taking care of ourselves
Conflict is going to happen no matter who we date. Everyone has triggers that get stepped on from time to time. What really matters is how we identify and communicate our needs and feelings, and how we take care of ourselves when we get triggered.

For example, you have an argument with your partner and something she says keeps playing over and over in your mind as the day goes on. It reminds you of a toxic situation with an ex, or from a family dynamic. Your stomach hurts, your head spins, you feel shaky. These are the physiological effects of stress and the chemicals released in our bodies during fight or flight. We can't control when our bodies get sent into stress mode, but we can refocus our attention away from the conflict and back toward self-love and self-acceptance. We can practice self-assertiveness by communicating our needs and feelings in an appropriate way. We can practice self-soothing techniques like tapping.

It's an opportunity to start over
Perhaps the biggest upside to conflict is that it is an authentic opportunity to reconnect in the relationship. Relationship experts say that healthy relationships go through natural cycles of break, repair, break, repair.

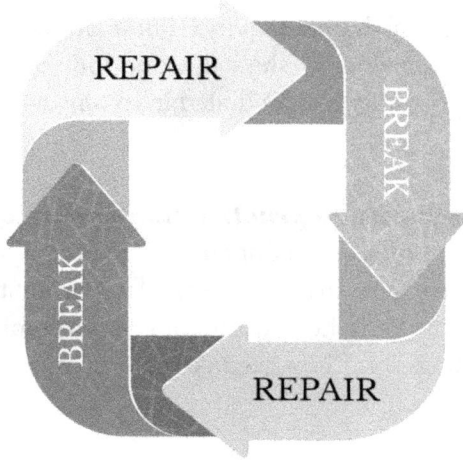

The breaks are conflicts, however minor. Repairs are the communication and reconnection patterns we use to come back together in intimacy. Without these repairs, relationships tend to grow apart, or become somewhat superficial, lacking depth and true connection that sustains love over time.

One powerful tool that supports us in all of our relationships is communicating during conflict. When we can beef up our communication and conflict-resolution skills, we are not only better able to tolerate conflict when it happens, but we can go back and repair when issues arise. This builds our intimacy muscle and helps us to trust ourselves and let go of the need to be perfect. It takes courage to have hard conversations, to bring up issues that we know created conflicts. One of the best ways to do this is to push past the need to avoid being a bad guy and saying the real thing rather than the polite thing to avoid uncomfortable feelings.

Navigating conflict in a healthy way means balancing the needs of the relationship with a healthy dose of self-love and self-assertiveness. While we may not always have this balance in check, reframing conflict from a bad thing to avoid to a natural, healthy opportunity to grow closer together is a good first step. For healthy relationships we need healthy habits. Establishing routines and habits that serve us are a good step.

—

RESOURCE TIP: For more information about healthy relationships, read *Conscious Loving: The Journey to Co-Commitment A Way to Be Fully Together Without Giving Up Yourself* by Gay and Kathlyn Hendricks.

Summary

We often lose sight of our healthy habits or we develop unhealthy habits when we get into a dating or relationship situation. This loss of focus happens because we are conditioned to ignore bad feelings, we are habitually unconscious, we fall into disempowered thinking, we lose alignment with ourselves, and we lack the tools and skills. The good news is that we can empower ourselves by practicing healthy habits daily. Acknowledging where we are, and course-correcting to establish routines and habits that serve us can turn it all around.

Dating and relationship baggage may be inevitable, but it doesn't have to control us. By healing the baggage of the past through processing stuck grief, taking responsibility for our part in relationships, and raising our self-awareness, we empower ourselves rather than living a victim story. Taking care of the present by valuing ourselves and identifying when toxic relationships develop helps us find ourselves again when we get lost in relationships. Finally, empowering our future by taking care of our own needs and practicing healthy habits sets the stage for all parts of our lives to improve. Uncovering the blocks that keep us stuck in unhealthy habits and refocusing our attention on developing a healthier relationship with the person who matters the most—ourselves—may be one of the most powerful practices in standing in our power as authentic women. Thank you for joining me on this journey.

Choose love.
Choose you.

References

Resources

Branden, N. (1994). *The Six Pillars of Self-Esteem: The Definitive Work on Self-Esteem by the Leading Pioneer in the Field.* New York, NY: Bantam.

Brach, T. (2010). *Meditations for Emotional Healing: Finding Freedom in the Face of Difficulty* [Audiobook].

Brown, B. (2017). *Braving the Wilderness: The Quest for True Belonging and the Courage to Stand Alone.* New York, NY: Random House.

Brown, B. (2010). *The Gifts of Imperfection: Let Go of Who You Think You're Supposed to Be and Embrace Who You Are.* Center City, MN: Hazelden.

Brown, N.W. (2008). *Children of the Self-Absorbed.* Oakland, CA: New Harbinger Publications.

Brown, S. L. (2010). *Women Who Love Psychopaths: Inside the Relationships of Inevitable Harm with Psychopaths, Sociopaths & Narcissists.* Minneapolis, MN: Mask Publishing.

Elliott, S. J. (2009). *Getting Past Your Breakup: How to Turn a Devastating Loss Into the Best Thing That Ever Happened to You.* Cambridge, MA: Da Capo Press.

Elrod, H. & S. Scott (2016). *The Miracle Morning for Writers: How to Build a Writing Ritual That Increases Your Impact and Your Income.* Hal Elrod International.

Hotchkiss, S. & J. Masterson (2003). *Why Is It Always About You? The Seven Deadline Sins of Narcissism.* New York: NY, Free Press.

Hendricks, G. & K. Hendricks (1990). *Conscious Loving: The Journey to Co-Commitment A Way to Be Fully Together Without Giving Up Yourself.* New York, NY: Bantam.

Horowitz, R. (2017). *How Can I Get Better? An Action Plan for Treating Resistant Lyme and Chronic Disease.* New York: NY, St. Martin's Press.

James, J. & R. Friedman (2009). *The Grief Recovery Handbook: The Action Program for Moving Beyond Death, Divorce, and Other Losses Including Health, Career, and Faith.* New York, NY: Harper-Collins.

Lerner, H. (2004), *The Dance of Fear: Rising Above Anxiety, Fear, and Shame to Be Your Best and Bravest Self.* New York: NY, Harper-Collins Publishers.

Ortner, N. (2014). *The Tapping Solution: A Revolutionary System for Stress-Free Living.* Hay House.

Scher, A. (2016). *How to Heal Yourself When No One Else Can: A Total Self-Healing Approach for Mind, Body, & Spirit.* Woodbury, MN: Llewellyn Publications.

About the Author

Kim Baker has been a dating and relationship columnist for over nine years. She writes for *Curve* and *Epochalips*, and is the author of *Girls' Guide to Healthy Dating: Between the Breakup and the Next U-Haul*. Her background in education and psychology have given her a lens of mindfulness and self-responsibility in writing about dating and relationships. Find her at www.girls-guidetohealthydating.com, on Twitter @gg2dating, or text gg2dating to 22828 to subscribe to her newsletter. *Message and data rates may apply.*

Also by Kim Baker

Girls' Guide to Healthy Dating: Between the Breakup and the Next U-Haul

Relationship Red Flags Mini Book

www.ingramcontent.com/pod-product-compliance
Lightning Source LLC
Chambersburg PA
CBHW060501280326
41933CB00014B/2811